Codger & Sweets

To Cindy,
The friend of the friendless and
the despenser of spiritual wisdom,

Thanks for shareing our journey

Codger Tom Donnelly

& Sweet Nancy

Thomas Donnelly

THOMAS DONNELLY

Final Version 11

©2016 Thomas Donnelly

ISBN: 978-1537093833

www.CodsgerandSweets.com

DEDICATION

Since the effort put into raising children birthed by another is harder than walking uphill backwards at midnight in a rainstorm, we would like to dedicate this book to all who have done so and kept small pieces of their sense of humor, as well as their marriage.

THOMAS DONNELLY

INTRODUCTION

The book you hold in your hands is not my fault. Writing is hard work, and I have spent a lifetime trying to avoid all forms of hard work. I blame it on all those people who have been reading my column for many years and have asked for the book to send to friends, thereby cutting down on the time spent on Christmas presents for distant relatives. I blame this book on Sweet Nancy, who let me know I owed her for numerous infractions through the years. "It should be fun and strengthen our marriage if we rewrote all the columns," I remember her saying early one morning before I was fully awake.

I blame publisher, John O'Melveny Woods, who in a moment of weakness or perhaps heartburn, agreed my work was worth publishing. He was willing to help me through the maze.

But most of all I blame the beginning on a sweet old lady, Judy, who asked me to write something for a filler in the newsletter of the Kearsarge Council on Aging in New London, New Hampshire. Nancy Friese, director of KCOA, who has a sweet spot for funny old men, encouraged me to keep writing, knowing that I cannot resist a strong woman who loves to ride horses while balancing a grandchild on the saddle.

The damage is done, the book is written; Sweets and I are still speaking to each other, and our work looks pretty good.

We hope, as you read, you will laugh, view life with more hope, and occasionally be touched by the stories of the people who allowed me to share their journey. I hope in our story you will be reminded of a story of your own and want to share it. Each and every story needs a teller and a listener. It works so much better if you take turns. It is in this joy-filled experience that life is richer and worth living.

Tom Donnelly, aka The Codger
Sweet Nancy, Censor and Editor

TABLE OF CONTENTS

Adventures with Sweet Nancy
and the Cranky Codger - 3

The 12 Days Hit squad - 5

My Hometown - 8

My Arms are my Legs - 10

Wicked Cold in Wintah - 13

Codger Scavenger Hunt - 15

Momma's Day - 17

Y'All Talk Funny, Bless Your Heart - 19

Finding Life's Magic Moments - 21

Where There a Will, There's a Way Out - 23

Thanksgiving, Living Thankfully - 25

Buying the Last Car? - 27

The Christmas Letter - 29

New Year's Revolutions - 31

My Phone and I - 33

Mid-Winter - 35

Meeting Mr. Tony - 37

Ask the Codger - 39

Fatherhood, Growing-up Time - 42

September 12th - 44

The Plane People - 46

Grandfather Power - 48

I Hate to Exercise - 50

The Artist Within - 52

Your Name is ??? - 54

Christmas Gifts - 56

Grandpa's Confusion - 58

(Sent from my Favorite Granddaughter) - 60

Dear Special Granddaughter - 62

The Little Librarian - 64

Cookies at Funerals - 66

The Strawberry Children - 68

The Season of Giving Thanks - 70

Television Makes you Fat - 72

Just Say the Words - 74

Small Town Christmas - 76

Get Out the Glue, Honey, I'm Falling Apart - 78

Critter Wars - 80

Notes from a Wrinkled Valentine - 82

Hibernating Among the Cobwebs - 84

Grady and the Guys - 86

It's About Time - 89

Stuff - 90

Our Littlest Valentine - 92

In the Land of OAPs - 94

Who is That Old Guy in the Mirror? - 97

The Art of Mothering - 99

I Wish I had Known Him - 101

Summer Memories - 103

The Johnny Appleseed of Music - 105

The Annual Christmas Clash - 107

Are You Smarter than Your Smart Phone? - 109

Flight of the Codger - 111

An Unhurried Life - 113

To My Sons - 115

Gaining Wisdom from

Random Acts of Stupidity - 117

Surviving Christmas - 119

I Always Finish - 121

Vintage Movies - 124

Life Lessons - 126

Preparing for Wintah! - 128

The National Day of Eating - 130

Spaghetti Love - 132

Momma Weather, Only the Best for You - 134

My Wife Married an Alien - 136

Climbing the Digital Mountain - 138

Family Reunions - 140

The Night I Stole the Christmas Tree - 142

Guys and the Love Month - 144

Now & Then - 146

My wife Left Me - 148

The Final Party - 150

Wooden Desk Days - 152

A Public Service Announcement - 153

That's Not Funny, Honey - 156

The Summer Jubilee - 158

Grandma Power - 160

In Search of the Perfect Gift - 162

International Grandchildren - 164

My Gosh, When Did I Become Elderly? - 166

Chosen Children - 168

In Case of Emergency - 170

Free Range Children - 172

Get out the Candles Darling, Ice Storm Ahead - 174

Big Papa - 176

Power of Small - 178

It Ain't That Bad- Guy Humor - 181

Day Pass into Women's World - 183

May I Suggest - 185

The Old Man and the Dark Haired Girl - 187

A Story for Christmas - 190

Codger & Sweets

THOMAS DONNELLY

Adventures With Sweet Nancy and the Cranky Codger

Road trip time again. Longer days, snow is gone, four good tires, and a full tank of gas. Sweet informs me there is a world of difference between the road trips of our youth when we just needed clean underwear, a couple of dollars, and on occasion, a map. Now that our kids tell us we are elderly, we must go to Map quest, Google Maps, Yahoo and learn to use a GPS that highlights the bathroom stops with icons of red toilets.

We bring lots of supplies: medications, sleep machine, snore pillows, a magnifying glass for two handfuls of maps, two pairs of glasses, a cell phone, three pounds of healthy veggie snacks, today's newspaper, and more medication. I swear my wife keeps hiding things that I want to pack, like old sneakers, and replaces them with dress shoes. What once took an hour, now takes two days. This year we purchased a GPS, a global positioning dictator that has the voice of a third grade teacher. When we turn the wrong way she sighs LOUDLY, and says, "Let's try again, shall we? Turn around and go back the correct way!"

At last, we are ready; a road trip like the old days. We start early, since we both have difficulty sleeping. Whoever has slept the most hours begins to drive, while the other sleeps. When we take road trips we find: one likes the radio, the other not; one likes fresh air, the other air conditioning; one can sleep in a moving vehicle, the other only occasionally; one drives the speed limit, the other five miles over the limit—or more. In each case, the driver decides, the other grumbles. How can such different people remain married, let alone take trips together?

It helps if one has a poor memory, so that one can't remember why the other is grumbling. It helps if you are able to distract, such as when I point out the beautiful flowers or the purple cow in the farmer's field. Sweet says things like, "I'm shocked, did you see that hussy walking down the street topless?" "Where, oh, where?" I cry! She tells me she was mistaken; but too late, I am distracted.

We play games like, "how many codgers do you see driving white SUV's," or "how many women do we see who let their dog drive." I like to play "how many miles can I get before I run out of gas," but Sweets keeps hitting my arm with her shoe until I pull in for gas. She likes to play, what is that car noise and can you fix it? Then we move into Did You. Did you turn off the hose to the washing machine, or did you lock the door and turn down the heat? We have been known to play for days.

Trapped in a steel box going at least fifty-five miles an hour, one of us will bring up a subject better left untouched, such as "Have you thought about how you want to be buried, and whom shall I invite to the funeral? Shall I send out invitations or call your brother Louie direct?" Or "Sweets, I'm thinking about taking our retirement funds and living on the beach, Ok?" We may be elderly but road trips have never been more fun.

The 12 Days Hit Squad

There are families who seem to live in eternal winter, never ever seeing the sun. They remind me of winter gardens, frozen and ignored, save for a few hard-core gardeners. For these families, December seems unusually cruel, surrounded by all the smells, lights, and sounds of Christmas. When we meet them, we often feel helpless; and some of us walk out of our way, or in the opposite direction. Really, what can we do in such situations?

This is a story of an unlikely band of people in an earlier time and place who made a difference for one family, one Christmas, when like today, times were really hard.

It all started over a cup of coffee, when several of us happened to meet in the local diner. Someone knew a family having major problems. Dad was unemployed, because the large corporation, for which he had worked, had recently moved south; he had benefits only until the end of the year. The teen-aged son had congestive heart failure and needed an operation. Mom, a teacher in the primary school, was recently diagnosed with breast cancer and was undergoing treatment. Happily, the daughter in the elementary school was fine.

In the background, some group was whining the carol, "Twelve Days of Christmas." How I hated that song! One woman suggested we could help this family by using a program she had read about in a magazine. Thus we formed what we dubbed, "The 12 Days Hit Squad!" There were six of us in all. Tim, a biker past his prime; Russ a local barber; Jimbo, a scripture quoting dentist; Sol, a non-practicing Jewish guy who claimed to provide balance to Jimbo; Shirley, a school secretary; Sweets, a nurse in case of injury; and yours truly in my pre-codger days.

We had a plan. The Hit Squad would deliver a gift to the family on the last twelve days before Christmas. On day one, we gave them a Christmas tree, and on day twelve, Christmas Eve, we gave them 12 ornaments. In between we allowed sweet treats, food for a holiday dinner, fruit, gifts, etc. The number of items given had to correspond to those of the song. Each member of the Hit Squad took two days, and delivered the gift of his or her choice.

All of this was to be done in secret. Neither the family nor anyone else was to know our identities. We would meet in six days to discuss problems and progress. Let the games begin!!!

At the next meeting, we found those who delivered on the first three days had it easy; but after that all lights were on in and outside the house, and noses were glued to the windows. We were forced to hit the house late at night or early in the morning. So far no one was caught! We were so excited by the creativity we used, we had trouble sleeping the rest of the week.

During the coming days we varied our times of delivery, tied mesh bags to trees, filled their mailbox, had strangers make deliveries, and worked in pairs, so one could create a diversion. We were like kids again. Was it legal to have so much fun and laughter?

Then it was Christmas Eve. The family and friends were on high alert. Despite close calls, the Hit Squad was pulling it off. One more time! It would take all our resources! A bold move was required - in daylight. Right after mail delivery, we placed an unbreakable ornament with an attached note typed in each neighbor's mailbox, (The boxes were located at the end of the street.) The note read, "Please deliver this ornament to the family living at (address followed). You will be rewarded with a smile. Thank you so very much. Signed, The True Spirit of Christmas."

We don't know how many neighbors came together to meet and help the family, but we have heard stories. We do know that six people all grew a little taller, and together we were able to create a little magic and love for one family that December. Today, when I hear the song, The Twelve Days of Christmas, I reach back in time, remember, smile and feel warm all over. Do you know someone who needs a little December magic? If you know five or more other people who want to make a difference, you too can create your own Hit Squad, feel warm despite the cold and walk a little taller.

Merry Christmas from Codger Tom and Sweet Nancy

My Home Town

Did you see the dead man singing? Singing in the graveyard in the Barn Playhouse's outstanding production of Our Town this past summer? He was the big man with the beard and the golden voice. His name is Michael, a member of our men's group. In the notes for the Thornton Wilder play about a fictitious New Hampshire town, Tom DeMille wrote, "It is performed once a day somewhere in this country or abroad." There is a universal chord that still threads through our lives that ties us to a play produced in 1938.

I wonder if the play touches a need in us for a place we can call home. A hometown is more than streets, stores, and streetlights. It's a place where you are known, and the people smile your name. It's where people watch your house when you are away. It's the neighbor who takes your kids to soccer practice, or your mother to the doctor. It's the guy who waves as he plows your driveway, and as a bonus, shovels a path to your door, because he knows you fell last winter.

A hometown is all this, and so much more. A hometown is like a marriage. It takes a long time to get to know each other, and there are lots of speed bumps to smooth out. Eventually, if you are lucky, you find a fit like those old shoes, or that shirt you love, but if you wear it, your wife will not be seen with you.

We have found we love the flavor of a place that celebrates its hospital with a parade, a town where business owners fund Concerts on the Green, and banks give you lunch served by the staff. On some chilly day, go visit my friend, Linda, who proudly displays two blue Excellence-in-Service awards, and be warmed by her smile. Take one of the endless supplies of

Lake Sunapee Bank pens; then ask her about rabbits. Up the street, visit Erin's Haircuts for Men, my barber, whose husband is our police chief. Does a good job too, according to the old men at the coffee shop.

Those of us who have a hometown, have a thousand stories of hometown life that shape our lives. I will finish with one that is deep and meaningful to me. It was our first winter, twelve years ago. We had a FOUR FOOT snowfall in one blow. I remember banging my head against the wall, praying for Jesus to part the snowdrifts. Sweets handed me a shovel instead.

The next day there was a knock on the door. It was my neighbor; he was going out of town, and he asked me to keep the driveway of our eighty-year old neighbor clear of snow. On the inside I said, "Oh no, not the woman who doesn't speak to me and has a license plate, YaBut. But I did, and Sweets and I became trusted friends of Franny. We grew to love her sassy ways and her devotion to her family dog and our town. Now, years later, her daughter and her husband live there. We are the older generation, and they care for us when needed, our guardian angels in so many ways.

This is a snapshot of my world and some of the people who have reached out, and in doing so, have given us a place for which we had been searching for so many years. Sit back and think about those who have been a part of the town you call home, and enjoy the warm glow from your neighbors, like us.

My Arms are my Legs

Each spring day I watch a caravan of cars circle the gym parking lot as I exercise behind a wall of windows, just above the handicapped parking. Walking on a treadmill, I observe a gray van slice off and pull into its usual spot. A slender woman with long brown hair reaches down to her right, lifts a walker, and in one motion, twists left, swings it over the steering wheel, down to the blacktop, and snaps it open. A difficult maneuver, one perfected by daily practice. She pulls herself up, and drops left down between the walker handles. Fascinated, I watch, as her arms will her body across the sidewalk, up the ramp, and into the gym. Time measured on the treadmill clock: twelve minutes. During the next four hours, she will swim, lift weights, row, and follow an exercise regime using the gym machines. She will sandwich in a physical therapy session before leaving to care for her grandchild at her daughter's house. She takes weekends and major national holidays off.

Her name is Pam Fischer, and she lives in Magnolia Springs, Alabama. Until four years ago, she was a long distance runner, and a customer service manager at a local bank. She had a pain in her leg she thought was sciatica due to running. However medical tests revealed a ten and a half inch tumor on her spine. December 11, 2012, the day of her ten-hour operation is burned into her memory. It was the last day she walked. She awoke the day after surgery unable to move. She was in ICU for three days, followed by three months in the hospital. She was told she would never walk again. She spent the next two years in a wheelchair. This fiercely proud woman was trapped in her wheelchair, and hated the thought this would be her future for the rest of her life.

Waiting in the shadows was the family, the foundation of recovery, so often forgotten. Her husband, Fred, her rock, had her back every step of the way. Her son and daughter were cheering, supporting, and praying. Most of all, precious Abigail, an infant, really needed her "Nam, Nam" to be part of her life. Pam could trust her doctors to know medicine, but they did not know her, or the power of her loving family.

She told me, "I could wallow in pity, or I could get angry." She chose the energy of anger to do her job. Her job was to "take care of my body, which is my hope for the future. I knew in my heart of hearts, the wheelchair was not the final stage. I knew there was something more, if not tomorrow, then a day in the future. I need to be ready!"

So she worked her way out of her chair. It was not easy. She struggled and worked; she still does, but she persists. It is a work in progress.

Pam doesn't have time to stop, so I sit next to her as she works out. I asked her what she wanted others to know about her path to recovering her life. She tells me she doesn't take pain pills. She still has down days, but they don't last as long. She wishes that others would see her as a PERSON with a disability because she is "so much more than her disability." She has a life outside her disability. For those of us who have the privilege of knowing her, we call her our inspiration to not give up and try a little harder. More than an inspiration she has become my friend. There are chapters yet to be written in Pam Fischer's story!

Wicked Cold in Wintah

As I inch toward maturity (old age), strange things are happening. At this time of the year, wintah, I look like a bowling ball with feet, as I shuffle across the frozen tundra. While I seek warm sunlight, a gray umbrella covers my town, New London. When I was younger, I wore a tee shirt and light jeans until the end of January. Now, I have an intimate relationship with anything made from wool. I have cold flashes, which feel like I swallowed an icicle. This is a Biological Climate Change of Biblical Proportions!

I am not alone. There are other codgers like me, although many try to remain hidden. You can identify them by their tendency to wear knit Patriot watch caps with matching heavy sweaters, sitting indoors next to the woodstove. A brotherhood begging for a short wintah, or an invitation from a southern friend.

Our wives, who for years wore hats, socks, and gloves to bed, have moved in the opposite direction, giving new meaning to the word, hottie. For example, Sweet Nancy and I will be driving home from a Dartmouth hockey game, held in an unheated arena. Suddenly she shouts, "I'm hot." Ignoring the snowstorm in which we are driving, she lowers all the windows. I reach into the back seat for the woolen blanket, crawl near the heater on the floor, wailing and dialing 911 for assistance. Who says that older couples lack excitement in their lives?

Still, with the rising costs of heating oil, sleeping in the same bed provides warmth all wintah. Our motto is: we cuddle because we must, spring is only six months away.

Till then, a warm greeting in the new year for all of you, and for those whom you love, hold them close for warmth and comfort. Look for the groundhog.

Codger Scavenger Hunt

My watch is lost—again. Three times this week that same watch has wandered away. It probably went looking for the pocket watch that's missing from the previous week.

I seldom tell Sweet Nancy about the watch's poor behavior, to save her from rolling her eyes and muttering incantations in ancient Greek and wailing, "What did you lose now?"

"Lose? I didn't lose anything," I calmly reply, "it's in the house—somewhere. There's no need to call the Codger Search and Rescue with their dog, Big Sniff! You've probably organized the area and me again, putting everything where I can't find it."

Despite the compliment I just paid her, she left the room slamming the door; leaving me to wonder if there is a Codger Lost and Seldom Found area, where one would finally find old sunglasses, check books, tools, pens, one sneaker, socks, and those letters written, but never mailed. It's a place where old men wander through supermarkets. In the back, there's a large parking lot filled with the sound of car electronic keys opening and closing locks. It's a room where there are shelves with dictionaries of lost words, volumes of unremembered names, and a large book with large gold letters, FORGOTTEN FRIENDS.

There are days when I just spend too much time searching. If I look too long, I find only despair, thinking "What's wrong with me or worse." Yet on the same day, I can easily remember the day I met my wife, the day I became a dad, and that big blue ribbon won at the show. I can remember the starting lineup of the Green Bay Packers on the day of the Ice Bowl, or Ted Williams' lifetime batting average. It all depends on your priorities. For every object I've lost, I can remember a client or a friend saying wonderful words, "You were there for me, thanks." Or even more special, "You helped me change my life, when everyone else had given up." Words and memories that lift instead of push down. We all have such memories; they're only a thought away.

As we age, I know some of us are vexed when we lose things. I am forever losing my glasses; that's why I have several pairs. I just need to never lose sight of what is important, family, friends, good food, and the gift of life. Besides I'm retired, what need do I have for a watch?

Momma's Day

When I was small and full of beans, my mother would frequently end the day beating her chest three times, looking toward the ceiling while pounding the table with a clenched fist. She would wail, "Sweet Jesus, Oh Sweet Jesus, please give me the strength not to wring his scrawny neck." Mom was quite a kidder.

I was a child of a thousand whys, and double that number on the "don't wanna" scale. Church people would call me "a trial" and a "test of faith." Neighbors would call me a "handful." My brother called me "the bad seed," and volunteered to take me deep into the woods. As you can see, he inherited Mom's sense of humor. Aunt Helen would put her large arm around Mom's small, bent frame, lean in, and whisper, "That boy is gonna need a flock of strong momma's and a posse of whip toting daddies. If he gets that, he might just make it to high school." My family was rolling in comedy writers!

I wonder if Mom tried too hard to keep me clean, and it just wore her out. I'm sure if I called her from some police station with my one free phone call, to tell her they were beating me with rubber hoses, and they had just pulled out paddles for electric shock treatment, she would say, "Are you wearing clean underwear? You know, in case you end up in the prison hospital?" My mother truly believed you were immune from harm if you wore clean underwear. If I told one of my occasional deviations from the truth, she would wash my mouth out with soap. If I scratched myself "down there," she would scrub my hands so clean I could perform surgery. As the wild child, I could blacken my face, rip my pants, hit my nose, and have it bleed on my shirt between the back door and the car, on my way to church. I didn't try to get dirty; it just was part of my DNA. Mom would clench her fists and mutter, "Someday, someday when you have children of your own ... "

I was unaware of the power of the mothers' curse until I had children of my own. One morning I discovered my oldest had poured maple syrup all over his cereal, which was heaped in a pile on the floor. As I gasped for breath, clenched my fists in a chokehold around his neck, I heard what sounded like my mother's laugh. I knew then it was my job to make sure he lived until high school. I just hoped my wife never found out the source of our curse. With a hairbrush, and a room full of mommas, I turned out fine; so could he, I hoped and prayed.

So there is absolutely no call for Sweets' behavior when she sits in the rocking chair, looks toward heaven, beats her chest three times, and murmurs; "Sweet Jesus, Sweet Jesus." Our children are adults now, who could upset her any longer?

Let's give a special toast for all the moms who raised to adulthood those of us who were a trial and a handful; a standing round of applause to them for not giving up. I know my own mother is in heaven, because I already put her through hell.

Y'all Talk Funny, Bless Your Heart

Southern women have mastered the art of strong opinion tempered by phrases sprinkled with sugar. Like this: a woman, frustrated with her son, although proud of his law degree said, "Makes y'all want to go home and kill that boy, bless his precious heart."

One of my favorite southern ladies is a woman I call Momma. I visited Momma at her son's business on Thursday, the one day she doesn't have a meeting scheduled, for she is a retired professional, and her skills and energy are still valued.

On this day in mid-February, temperature forty degrees, deep in the heart of Dixie, she is wearing a full-length fur coat. "Good Lord, it's so cold my nostrils snapped shut. I can't take it anymore. I just cannot understand how those northerners can stand it. I saw on television they have SNOW. DEEP KILLER SNOW! How can they live like that? It's just pitiful."

I replied, "I think the birth rate goes up, maybe just to keep warm."

"Is that a fact? I always wanted to ask when they come into the store, but I can't understand their accents; they talk funny."

We talk funny? We have accents that are hard to understand? Did Momma forget I was a New Hampshire Yankee, or was she just funning me? Thus began my experiment of trying to pass. I went to BB&T (Best Bank in Town) to begin my experiment.

"Morning Miss Edith, Miss Valerie. How y'all doing? Is Miss Becky takin' care?" (All are married women, one as I write, with child.)

Walking down the street I would see men with a large A on their caps (for University of Alabama), and I'd say, "Roll

Tide." They gave me a weak grin, or turned away confused. I felt like the village idiot. What had I done wrong?

I met JT (his name, not his initials), thin, lanky, and with a drawl so long you have to sit down when he just said hello. I told him of my experiment. "Am I not pronouncing the words correctly? Is it my (gulp) accent?"

In the interest of saving a tree, I will interpret his response as, "Nope."

"Well," I asked, "What is it?"

JT responded, "Well, I guess it is the dead on fact that you wear a Boston Red Sox cap."

"Oh. Yeah."

I have noticed there is a type of litmus test involving pronouncement of words and regional foods in many parts of our country. Sweet Nancy's brothers in Wisconsin asked me to pronounce Manitowoc, and did I like brats? My New Hampshire neighbors asked about Concord, pronounced Conca'd, and had I eaten pontine? In 'Bama I noticed school, pronounced with long vowels, scho-o-ol; hey instead of hello, followed by asking me what church would I be attending on Sunday and where did I like my Bar-B-Q?

I know these are tests, but what I don't know is: are the tests to invite me in, or to keep me out? And why should I care?

Finding Life's Magic Moments

On the gulf coast there is a path some call the Mardi Gras highway. It begins at Mobile, Alabama, stretches west along the coast to end in New Orleans. Television and the internet have provided a distorted view of Mardi Gras as a drunken orgy where people dress in masks and bright costumes in order to hide bad behavior, and drugged, naked college girls dance on Creole balconies.

That may be true for New Orleans. But I would like to present a different family-friendly view, as practiced in Daphne, Alabama and other shore communities along the Gulf Coast. This Mardi Gras, orgy-free, is seen through the eyes of my friend, Billy Jones. For most the year, Billy is a respected, professional sign language interpreter for the Mobile Public School system. During carnival he is Captain Jack Sparrow, a member of the pirate krewe, Shadow Barons. (A krewe is a club that sponsors a float for the Mardi Gras parade and formal ball.)

The official start of Mardi Gras season is forty-seven days before Easter, but Billy and the other krewe members prepare for it most of the year. Billy's eyes dance with excitement as he warms up to his favorite subject. "It's a celebration by everyday people for everyday people. My wife, Kathy, goes all out for Christmas; this is my Christmas."

One of the differences is that Billy's carefully selected gifts are thrown from the top of a moving float, shaped like a pirate ship, to people five deep along the parade route waving their arms and calling, "Throw me something!" Billy goes on, "We are a band of brothers from all walks of life joined together to give the community something special, using our sweat, muscle, and own money." Billy throws out sixteen boxes of unique beads as well as other throws. His personal cost starts at $1,000 dollars a year, a line item in his salary.

He continued, "What makes it all worthwhile for us, is that magic moment when we connect with someone in the crowd. One year I noticed a small girl lost in a sea of bigger kids. When she caught the large teddy bear I tossed her, I took home the warmth of her smile and the excitement of her laughter. Another year, it was a bent old lady in a lawn chair, with a shawl draped across her lap. I spied her, put a strand of large white beads in a cup with a lid, and tossed it underhand into her lap. She opened it, jumped up, and let out a yell. It was beautiful! For most of us the magic moments can make us feel good the rest of the year." Billy sees those among us who are unseen or ignored. He continues his gifting on Sunday in his church by signing for those who cannot hear.

The end of Mardi Gras comes on Fat Tuesday or Pancake Day, often at the end of the long winter. It is the day before Ash Wednesday. In carnival time, as in life, our thirst for more light is satisfied when we connect with others in our community and feel the warmth. Then it is a new season; people, like plants, search for sunlight for new growth. It's time for the people to parade outside into the sun of springtime.

Where There's a Will, There's a Way Out

"Thomas? Tho-o-mas, where are you?"

"Why is she using my trouble name? Used only on special occasions, such as when I have run over her new flower with the lawnmower, or when she thinks I have forgotten a minor detail like paying the electric bill. If I can make it down to my workshop where it's so messy she communicates only from the edges, I'll be safe."

My wily wife knows my ways and cuts off my escape route. "Thomas, we need to make a will!"

Codger: "A will? What is it you are not telling me? I thought my last lab tests were fine. Besides I thought we both had wills."

Sweet Nancy: "This is not about you. That will was written ten years ago. We now live in dangerous times. There is swine flu, terrorists, climate change, and Congress. I want to make sure my plants get a good home. You get the house and the doctor bills, but my plants need love, plus someone who will remember to water them." This last emphasized with the killer wife's glare.

I thought, "Good grief, fifteen years ago, an African violet died under my watch while she visited her sister. She never forgets!"

Codger: "Tourists, why should I be afraid of those summer people? They've been coming here for years without a problem. We don't have any swine that I am aware of, and climate change? Just because it rains every three days? I do believe a yard full of mushrooms adds character to our lawn."

Sweets: "Thomas, not only do you have a hearing problem, you are again avoiding the issue. If by some freak accident we

23

both get hit by a runaway recreational vehicle while avoiding that yellow motor scooter from around town, do you want some stranger making medical decisions for us?"

Codger: "There you go, listening to those high paid know-it-alls on talk radio. Why just last year, a lady from New London Hospital came to our Monday morning Men's Group to tell us about something called an Advanced Directive, legal in the U.S. and some foreign countries. It seems you can, in advance of needing it, choose whom you want to make those decisions. She'll even help you fill out the forms."

Sweets: "So when did you fill out the forms, and did you bring me the forms as well? Thomas! Thomas! Now where did that man disappear?" Opening the door to the cellar, she called, "We need to talk about that will before I kill you myself for terminal stubbornness!"

Thanksgiving, Living Thankfully

"My name is Rusty," said the tall, bent man at the front of the room, dressed in jeans and a flannel shirt. "Everything I own of any importance is in this shoe box. I am a grateful alcoholic, and I have cancer. The docs gave me six months to live a year ago, so each day I am above the grass is a gift. I am a man living with two diseases, not dying of them, one day at a time. Everyday I have a choice to live flat out, or to get depressed about the end of my life.

"I live alone, but I am seldom lonely because of what's in this box. In this box are a Bible, the AA Big Book, and an address book with names and phone numbers of the people who are my gas stations. You see, when I am angry, lonely, or scared, I make a phone call. If the first person isn't home, or is out of gas, I call the next person. I find that I get something from each person, sometimes a little, sometimes enough to fill me up. At the end of each day I make a gratitude list. The list helps me stay off the pity pot. Tonight I am full, and I want to share my story to give you and me strength and hope."

The above took place over thirty-five years ago on a cold November evening, at a meeting of Make Today Count, a support group for people and their families living with a terminal illness. After Rusty spoke, gentle Peggy spent the next hour teaching a desperate man what it was like for a woman to live with breast cancer. She was a shining star in a dark time in my life.

This experience led my late wife, Viola, and me to starting our own chapter of Make Today Count, so that their caring and hope could be passed on. The group in turn was there for me at the end of Viola's journey.

Most of us don't live to this age without a significant loss. Some of us have many losses. There's the loss of sight, hearing, movement, and strength. Some of us have to give up driving, or our homes. Some of you, like me, lost a spouse which is like a hole in our soul; we had planned to grow old together. We older people can develop a hardening of the HEARTERIES; we no longer feel joy. We see this time of thanksgiving as false advertising, something to sell us, something from corporations.

Rusty had his gas stations. I have my shining stars, which seem to glow when life is the darkest. Sometimes I have my eyes closed and can see nothing. My guess is that you have a few shining stars glowing in your lives; they may be in your own house like mine. Or they're maybe just a phone call away; but WE have to make the call.

As my friend Big Ed says, "If you want to change your attitude, focus on gratitude. If you look closely at all those self-made men, they left out a few parts. I need a few good friends to tell me when I'm driving into a ditch."

Buying the Last Car?

After fifteen years and 200,000 miles of hard roads, the Sweetsmobile had almost as much wear as Uncle Edgar, who has been replacing essential body parts for years. Like Sweets' car, he now requires constant maintenance.

Focused like a laser, Sweets began—The Search. She had a three ring binder, six-hundred sheets of notebook paper, and recent auto brochures. She spent hours consulting the internet, Consumer Report's Annual Car Issue, Car and Driver Magazine, and Honest Fred's Sweet Deals/Hurricane Leftover Manual, three thick volumes. Wars between nations have been conducted with less planning and gnashing of teeth.

We consider purchasing a car equivalent to a root canal gone wrong. Bravely armed with our research and a firm resolve, we left our safe house to do battle with our evil nemesis, the car salesman, whose mission seemed to be to take advantage of innocent old people, like Sweets. Ouch! Ouch! I mean like us. Little did we realize we were not going to purchase a car, but instead were to find a new way to enhance our digital experiences.

As we entered the battleground, the salesman led us to his enhancement desk. Using his computer, he displayed an array of electronic wizardry featured in the car he was selling, including a virtual drive. I missed some of it, as my eyes had glazed over after the first fifteen minutes. Coming out of the trance, I inquired, "Do we ever get to drive this thing?"

"Sure," he answered, "after we get back the information from your insurance company, State Police criminal division, three banks, one government official, a member of the clergy, and two sober neighbors." In his defense, the salesman was young. I thought the crack in his voice amusing, but after four hours, car shopping was wearing our few remaining nerves thin. After the test drive we called halt, in order to go home to take a required recovery nap.

We returned two days later, to be met by a salesman with less hair than I had and complaining the weather was affecting his arthritis. Unlike the younger salesman, he considered computers a necessary evil, and took us to an actual car to show us its features. He and Sweets talked gardens, flowers, and exchanged photographs of our families. Since we had recently pledged our loyalty to God and Country, he took us for a test drive. He asked Sweets what she needed in a car and waited for her answer.

What sold her on this car was its backup camera, which enables her to back up like her brother Richie, the truck driver, plus the salesman's ability to keep her paper bag filled with popcorn, something she loves almost as much as sunshine. Now, which salesman do you think made the sale?

We have reached the age where we ask, "Is this our last car purchase?" We know we have over 200,000 miles left in us, but will the warranty on our parts run out before then? Only time will tell. Now, where did Sweets hide those keys? There's a new toy in town, calling my name.

The Christmas Letter

Every year we receive end of the year/holiday letters from far away friends, family, and foes; some who feel compelled to inform us of their wonderful life. I know some of them leave out a few of the year's most challenging moments. Can you imagine a full disclosure dispatch, like the following, from one of these folk?

Dear (fill in your name):

I do hope that you and your family are doing better than the little woman and me. As you will recall, we moved to Florida to escape New Hampshire winters. It seems that every third geezer on the East Coast had the same idea. You have never seen such fender benders and traffic snarls. These old folks cannot see, even in daylight, and they travel in caravans at twenty miles an hour.

No one warned me about the six-month summers. Ninety-five degrees on a cool day, with two hundred per-cent humidity. We have a service that power washes the moss off our house EVERY MONTH! We go out before the sun rises, then come home, and spend the day in our cool cellar. We do not leave until the sun goes down. We feel we are in a witness protection program.

Then there is the prehistoric wildlife to guard against. These creatures crawl out of roadside gullies and storm sewers, so we don't walk anywhere. Would you believe bugs as big as soft balls? With beady eyes and fangs. Mean, attack bugs! They suck blood, so we wear long sleeves all year! Thank heavens the snakes and vampire bats keep their population down.

Our son's family is much improved this year, since his wife found a job with insurance benefits. It even covers most of his treatment for depression. Mother thinks his condition was brought on by having to train foreign replacements for his last five jobs that were outsourced. The language barriers certainly didn't help. I don't know about those things, since I worked for the same company twenty-five years before taking early retirement.

We are certainly doing much better financially, since we no longer have to pay most of our grandson's tuition that was not covered by scholarships from MIT. It took a few months, but he finally has secured a management position at a company called Mickey D's. I don't know what they manufacture, but he assures me it can't be exported, so that's good. His sister, Heliotrope, due to the poor economy, is forced to work nights. I think it has something to do with motels or is it hotels? Perhaps this is also due to her decision to leave Princeton in her senior year, and enroll in a program at the Betty Ford Clinic. Personally, I think this was a mistake; she would have been much better off getting her degree first. Little wonder she has to work all night with that attitude. Her grandmother prays for her daily.

Well, it's dark now, and time to find a place that is serving an Older Timers Special. Say hello to the Missus and happy holiday to you both.

Signed:

Smiley and Herself

New Year's Revolutions

"Grandpa, what's a New Year's Revolution?" asked the small boy of a large man who was holding him on his lap. "Well, Jack," said the laughing man, "it's a promise you make to yourself which you keep about a month. The next year you make the same promise again and expect things will be different that year. That's why it's called a revolution, it keeps revolving."

I made the same revolution regarding my weight for decades. During my lifetime I have lost the combined weight of three musk oxen, as well as a small mountain goat. I always gained it all back, and blamed it on a separate entity, my stomach, that I called Friendly Fred. It was a pillow, first for my kids and then for my grandchildren. I convinced one grandchild to have a conversation with Fred. She would pat Fred and say good-bye to him, not me. It was a kid magnet, how could I let him go?

Today because of the advantage of my advanced age, I am at my correct weight. I have laid off Omar the Tentmaker and can bend down and tie my shoes. I can rise out of chairs without using the arms of the chair and a rope pulley, or the aid of a hydraulic lift. A really big deal for me! How did I do it?

Due to AA (advanced aging) I developed a swallowing problem that prevented me from swallowing a Big Whopper in two bites. I actually chewed and tasted food, which made me realize I didn't really like big greasy sandwiches, and I knew when I was full. Normal people know when they are full. I didn't and couldn't say no to the lure of more. Cardiac problems gave me a stent, sentencing me to the Dartmouth Cardio Boot Camp where they trained me for the Geezer Olympics. I learned a portion was the size of Sweet's clenched fist, not basketball player, Shaq O'Neil. It was there that those formerly nice women sent a note home to Sweets advising her that red meat, added salt, and fatty foods were forbidden. I became aware that one of anything was not enough for Fred, but any more was too much for me. Sweets and I both lost weight, as well as lowering our blood pressure.

Prior to stumbling on the Advanced Aging Advantage (AAA), I had been to Lean Line, the Fat Guys Drink Beer & Wine Quick Loss, Overeaters Anonymous (where I learned about my addiction to certain foods), and finally Weight Watchers. At WW I finally learned it was crazy doing it my way, which didn't work, and expecting different results. By following the program, and armed with AAA, I lost the pounds and kept them off.

AAA can help in other ways such as saving money. One woman told me because of poor memory she buys one book and just rereads it, saving both time and storage space. Think of the possibilities, one exercise video, one television channel, the list is endless. I wonder if I can use AAA when I am audited for taxes. After all, I am of an advanced age, how can I remember to have receipts? I could save money on presents, insult strangers, make claims without proof, like politicians. What fun!

May your revolutions become resolutions; it's never too late to have fun.

My Phone and I

A few months ago my eight-year old flip phone broke into three pieces. I needed a simple replacement. At the same time, Sweet Nancy's too darn smart phone was misbehaving, so we made a double date at the local store of America's Most Reliable Network, Period. Verizon. On some days, as reliable as two paper cups with a string pulled tight between them. This was during the Christmas shopping season, when women with too much money, were buying smart phones for their children.

At the store, I waited while the tech helped Sweets. As the women made their purchases, they sat next to me, and gave a mini commercial for smart phones with more passion than a teen-aged girl at a Justin Bieber concert. I was amused, but detached, until the third woman, wearing perfume that smelled like apple pie, my favorite, sat next to me. After a commercial delivered in a slow southern voice thick as corn syrup, she turned to me, stunned me with her smile, and said "So, Sugah, what kind of phone y'all buying today?" The next thing I remember was Sweets shaking my shoulder, "Well, have you decided what kind of phone are you going to buy?"

I answered from a far away place, "I'll have one of those blue smarty phones." I heard my mother's voice, "Don't forget there are starving children in Africa." I ignored the voice, wrote a check, and walked off into a life of sinful indulgence. Later I realized the phone cost more than my first car. I hope it runs better.

My phone and I have not become friends. Some days I yearn for my old phone. I know some folks treat their phone as a body implant, much like a knee replacement, necessary for life. I have read that people check their phone 130 times a day.

I am old, but I have so much more to do than check my phone. My people go on vacation to get away from telemarketers and political surveys, not invite them for dinner.

I reluctantly admit there are advantages. Sweets maintains contact with our scattered family who refuse phone calls, but answer texts within minutes. I can find Sweets in a grocery store. The phone shows the location of rest stops on the interstates, cheap gas, places to eat, and emergency hospitals. It even shows the place where I am lost, and how to find my way home.

I know I am not alone in my battle with modern times. Technology can make our lives easier, or stain our faces with tears of frustration. At times like these, we need a child who can lead us toward the light. Ideally he or she is a grandchild, so the hourly rate is within our budget. I am waiting for the day when our cars drive us to our destination, while I nap in the backseat. Until then…

Mid-Winter

"In the bleak mid-winter, frosty wind made moan, earth stood hard as iron, water like a stone." Sounds like winter in New England. An English poet, Christina Rosetti, wrote these words about 1872. Later set to music, it's now considered to be one of our most revered carols, as determined in a poll of the world's choirmasters.

Christmas seems so long ago, although I scored a bull's eye with Sweets' Christmas present. It had been painful watching her saw the winter wood supply with a handsaw, so I went all out and bought her a 24-inch chainsaw. Obviously, such a caring gesture stunned her into silence. She has not spoken to me since that day.

I know we have reached mid-winter, because young people are wearing long pants, and my neighbor, Paul, wears a sweatshirt outdoors, and it's not even snowing. Now is the time we in New Hampshire enjoy the silence, a silence known only in winter. We experience a taste of wonder when we slip outside after a soft snowfall. Walking into a crisp winter night, we hear the sound of our boots sinking step by step along our dooryard path.

Once there was a night, pulled down from my shelf of memories, when I looked through my frosty windows, and saw in the heavens a ghostly glow with streaks of green, silver, and red. Some call it the northern lights, yet for me, it was so much more. I saw the winter fireworks display of New England, and heard the sound of silence. As the world slows, sighing, we watch our breath hanging in the night air.

Kim, my dental technician, and one of the singing Lowe sisters, called the Lowe Profiles, loves winters. She scolds anyone who complains about cold and snow. She tells me it is the time of Gandolf (from Lord of the Rings) coming down from the mountain. He wears his long robe, and moves his wand, spreading stillness and soft white beauty across our world. She invites the yearly coming, so her family can sail across the whiteness, winter sailors following the wind.

Sweets is a winter person; it was not always so. Somewhere our paths switched. She has joined the natives; in January she wears jeans and an unbuttoned light jacket. I resemble a young child in a snowsuit, wool hat, with a two-foot long scarf wrapped around, so only my beady eyes are visible. However, her winter joy draws the line at snow blowers. She tells me, "I will shovel a path to our door for the mailman, friends, and lost children. In winter the couch is not your friend. Man up, and clear the driveway."

Perhaps it is the medication, or my age that chills me as the sun goes down. Sweets is singing, pointing out birds at the feeder, while I am sinking into a down comforter, dreaming of long days and sunlight. Mid-winter, the time for long naps, and dreaming of far away places with white sand beaches covered in warm sunshine. I hear my name whispered on the wind, "Codger, come to me, come to me," or is that me singing through my nose, again? Curled up, I begin to ponder in the frost-filled night about winter's gift of time, when chores can be delayed another day. The time to finish that book, the time to write to your far away grandchildren, the time to call an old friend, but most of all, the time to stand still and look around, counting your blessings.

We hope the next year brings you laughter, good health, and new friends.

Meeting Mr. Tony

He was a small man, buried deep in sheets and blankets in a large hospital bed. I wasn't sure he was there until the blankets moved. "Tony, are you awake? I'm from Patient Education; the nurses and your wife, Elizabeth, wanted me to visit you." (His future was dim, and they thought he was depressed.)

"Go away, I'm a-tired. What you want?"

Growing up in an Italian neighborhood, I knew something about the culture, so I asked, "How's your garden?" He shot up in the bed. "She's a-terrible! No rain, and the damn-a doctors keep me here. No can water!" Thus began my all too brief relationship with Mr. Tony, a retired, skilled pattern maker who had two loves, his gardens and his wife, Elizabeth. They had no children, and all his relatives were in Sicily. When he married Elizabeth, he became a U.S. citizen, and he left his homeland behind forever.

I called him Mr. Tony, because in the neighborhood, this was a sign of respect for someone old. Mr. Tony was in and out of the hospital, and each time I received a call to visit. He held my hand, and despite my protest that my people did not hold a man's hand, he would not let go. I learned to judge the amount of pain he was having by the pressure on my hand.

On his last trip home, Elizabeth called; Tony wanted to see me and my wife, so he could take us on a tour of his gardens. Of course we went. He had the longest and tallest grape arbor we had ever seen, as well as a tomato patch lush enough to feed the entire town. "To-o-m, I have-a present for you. You gonna love it. I know-a you gonna take good care." So I became the dubious owner of a night blooming cereus, a rare plant from a rare man. It was his pride and joy, like a child he never had.

Every year for years after, when the time was right, we called all our friends and shouted, "Tonight's the night, bring your favorite wine for the toast." We all gathered in the middle of our yard, where sitting on a large platform, was a huge plant with fragrant blossoms as big as dinner plates. The sweet smell filled the neighborhood for one night only, and we held our glasses high to toast life, friendship, and the small Italian man with a big heart.

Mr. Tony and the night blooming cereus are long gone. I've since learned to awkwardly hold the hand of grandsons. Every year at the end of summer, when there's a certain smell, I inhale deeply, and remember to savor the small moments we have today, and to visit the places we almost forgot that feel like home.

Ask the Codger

High on a mountaintop in the snowcapped mountains, in the shadow of Mt. Kearsarge, sits the meditation retreat of the wise old guy who spends days without internet, trying to solve life's mysteries. The following is a sample of his answers to those seeking his wise counsel.

Dear Codger,
How do I apply for the latest government bailout called Cash for Codgers? My codger is cranky, and he's hard to get started.
Weary in Wilmot

Dear Weary,
I'm sorry; the program has been cancelled due to the troubled economy. The demand for codgers by rich Florida widows has dried up. I suggest you go to a local branch of Rent-A-Grandchild, and lock your crank and the child in a room filled with toys (not electronic). Have the child invite your Codger to play, and let the inner sweet granddad come out. Caution: Do not try to help. The process may take hours and if you intervene, the process is reset to the beginning.

Dear Codger,
Why don't men ask directions? My husband gets lost and we ride around for hours. I feel like a prisoner in a steel box since he will not stop the car for any reason.
Trapped in New London

Dear Trapped,

Buy him a GPS that features the voice of a drill sergeant; the one that says, "HEY PEABRAIN! PULL OVER AT THE NEXT GAS STATION!" He will claim he was going to stop anyway, and will rush to the restroom. Meanwhile, you slip the mechanic a ten spot, ask him to take your husband over by the tires and the grease pit, and give him directions. Garage smells lower a man's resistance, and advice coming from a car guy is more trusted the world over.

If this fails, use plan B. Since you are a prisoner, you have the right to carry a concealed weapon and shoot your way out. This is guaranteed to get his attention. *

* The last suggestion only applies if you are in New Jersey, and the incident occurs between midnight and five AM, on days that begin with the letter R.

Dear Codger,

No matter how I plead, beg, or threaten my husband, he refuses to put the seat down on the toilet. There is nothing so shocking as answering the call of nature in the middle of the night only to discover an icy rim, particularly in winter. Why is my man so insensitive?

Frosted in Sutton

Dear Frosted,

Some men believe they are the masters of the bathroom, since the room is often called by the male name, the John. Of course this is an illusion. If we males truly owned the bathroom, it would be painted gray, brown, or dark blue. There would be a beer or wine cooler on one side and a magazine rack on the other. There would also be a high definition television tuned to a sports channel across from his throne. Does this describe your bathroom? Of course not! I suggest you call your brother, Louie, and bribe him with a home cooked meal and a few six-packs. Ask him to hook up a motion sensitive light turned on by falling water, and activated by leaving the lid up. I'm sure this will let him see the light and remind him, particularly if you alert the neighbors to call the police if they suddenly see a bright light in the middle of the night.

Please note: The wise guy is no longer replying to snail mail. Due to the ravages of aging, he cannot stand the ever-present cold winds on the mountain. He now has a Twitter and Facebook account, and makes occasional public appearances in warm libraries followed by heavy doses of coffee.

Fatherhood, Growing Up Time

Guys, do you remember when you first became a father? I remember I was sitting in awkward confusion with a bunch of other men, all trying to avoid eye contact, when a nurse pointed a cattle prod at me and chirped, "It's a boy, congratulations!" At that moment the room began to spin, and my lost childhood flashed before my eyes. I must have turned green, because an older man, a father of five, squeezed my shoulder, leaned in and rasped through whiskey breath, "Don't worry lad, it will get easier with experience!"

With my first family of three biological children, I was a Father-in-Training. My oldest still has a slight limp from the diaper pins I pushed into his hip. I was better with the second group of three. Their mother was so good, that I shone in her reflection. She gave us all a strong sense of family before she passed to that special part of heaven reserved for moms. When the next four entered my life, I regressed.

Fortunately Sweet Nancy kept her sanity among the chaos. Sheer numbers had pushed the family past the tipping point, and Sweets began to carry a stun gun for protection. I, on the other hand, began to pray out loud between hallucinations, wear earplugs, and search the yellow pages for exorcists.

We went to family therapy, but after six sessions the therapist quit her profession to become a karate instructor. To survive, we contacted the Navy Seals and received advanced survival training. We took shifts at parenting, so the other could take long naps. We learned to consider caffeine a basic food group. That whiskey breath father of long ago lied through his teeth. Fathering didn't become easier. On some days it was hard to remember my own name, rank, and serial number. I was just Susan's, John's, Mike's etc. old man. Just when we thought we had raised the last one, they began to come back. They found it was easier and cheaper to find their true calling from home. We finally rented a PO Box and moved three times without a forwarding address. I suggested we change our last name, but Sweets said she had done that once, and never again.

Memory is a funny thing. These many years later, Sweet Nancy remembers her parenting years with fondness. When she tells her friends about this time, I wonder where was I during all that fun. I must admit the children grew up and became fine adults, mostly. Yet on this Fathers' Day, I will hum a few lines from the old Jerry Butler song, sung by Elvis, "Only the Strong Survive." It was about a man who was following the advice of his Momma. "Oh you got to be a man, you've got to take a stand, only the strong survive."

We showed up, we did our best, we freely gave our love, and now is the time to collect our hard earned rewards, GRANDCHILDREN! Life is good, tell them funny stories about their parents, lie if you must, watch the look of shock, have fun!

September 12th

Every September I have wanted to go back in memory to 2001, to 9/11, and share an event I witnessed that gave me a small seed of hope after that tragic day.

He was a regular at a men's group I ran in New Jersey. Some of the guys called him New York, because he fought his way out of Hell's Kitchen and gang life. I think it was because of his attitude, his swagger, and the way he growled his words in your face when he thought you messed up. He was also the kind of guy who covered your back in a fight, or drove you to the hospital in the middle of the night after the governor closed the roads in a snowstorm. He was a "You stop me? You and how many in your army?" kind of guy.

Six days a week he climbed high above New York City on the bridges where the wind never stops. He bossed a rugged crew of men who repaired and replaced defects on those huge highways of steel. It paid well enough for him to have a home and a family in the country, where the schools were good, and there was room for dirt bikes for his kids. In his spare time he made knives out of worn out auto springs, knives so well made, collectors waited years to own one.

He was on the bridges the day the planes hit the towers. He climbed down to go there, but couldn't make it through the flames of hell until September 12th. Then he and his crew walked through smoldering ashes, kneeling to sift for remains with their bare hands, 12 hours a day, 7 days a week, until they couldn't go on any longer. In rest times they found a corner to sleep, a pair of clean socks and underwear, and hot food to scarf down. These are the men, everyday people, who left their jobs to work through the pain and toxic dust until the job was done. He was one of them.

Like so many of you, I remember September 11th. I watched for hours, trying to make sense of the evil, as the TV replayed the planes hitting the towers. I felt the wind go out of the world. I walked outside, numb, wondering why the sun was still shining. In the distance I heard children laughing and playing, and for some strange reason I saw a small light of hope. The hope many of us felt on September 12th, when help came from every corner of our nation to begin the healing.

Every September, as a reminder, I unwrap a small knife given to me, made from a rusted car spring. It reminds me of a man I once knew, who gave me hope when I felt only fear. The same man who gave a steel cross, cut out of a beam from one of the towers, to his small country church. It reminds the people they are not alone, no matter how heavy the burden. I still wonder why it takes a tragedy of biblical proportions to put aside our differences to bring us together.

To be continued.

The Plane People

Last month I wrote about a man who gave me a small seed of hope after 9/11. This month I want to share a story about a small town in Canada that gave hope to almost 7,000 strangers. On September 11, 2001, all aircraft flying toward the United States were ordered to return to their point of origin, or find an airport and land as soon as possible, because of a terrorist attack. For the first time in history, the skies of our country were empty of aircraft. Thirty-eight planes carrying just shy of 7000 people landed in Gander, Newfoundland, a town of 10,000.

Newfoundland has it's own time zone, not shared with another country. Gander, due to its unique location was known as the gas station to the world, a major refueling and repair station during WW II and after, until non-stop trans-Atlantic flights became the norm. The resulting decline in air traffic created an unemployment rate of 16 per cent. Gander has also been called the lifeboat of the North Atlantic. A title earned once again on that day of terror. With thirty-eight planes landing, the call for help went out, and within hours, Gander, along with the surrounding area, formed a volunteer army.

First in line, the women of the Royal Canadian Legion stayed up all night making sandwiches to hand to passengers when they finally were allowed to leave their planes with only the clothes they were wearing. Next, striking bus drivers came off the picket line, and drove yellow school buses to transport deplaned passengers to shelters, some thirty miles away. Royal Canadian Mounties, allowed to pass through security, delivered free cigarettes to people trapped on the planes suffering withdrawal.

During the following days, pharmacies provided free medication for passengers with chronic conditions. Restaurants, service clubs, and churches served thousands of meals; no one went hungry. The townspeople fed people home cooked meals, and gave them sheets and towels from their own homes, without thought of their return. The plane people were invited into private homes to shower, but also to get away from the constant noise of so many people crowded together. The people of the planes were not treated as strangers, but rather as long lost relatives. Gander put its own life on hold to provide kindness to weary and worried strangers.

For this story, I interviewed a woman with a pixie smile, a former resident of Gander, who took time from her busy day to let me know that in Gander, kindness is a way of life. I watched a video about Operation Yellow Ribbon, and read the heart- warming book, "The Day the World Came to Town," by Jim Defede. He fleshes out the whole story. I have never been to Gander, but it is on my bucket list. I want to meet such kind-hearted people, and thank them for what they did for my fellow Americans. It is my hope each year as we remember the pain and fear of the terrorist attacks, we also remember a small town that reached across the miles in friendship, and in a small way sought to make the world a better place.

Grandfather Power

I am the resident old person of my blended family. I have many names, primarily due to the language ability of small children. In the New Jersey branch, I am known as Tasha; in Montana I am Boppa; in New Hampshire I am called Grandpa T; and in California I am just Grandpa. Put them all together, and they spell Grandfather.

Grandfather-hood can give us men a second chance. During the time when, out of necessity, we focused on earning a living, and were out of the house so much, we spent less time and energy on our children. With grandfather-hood we can balance the equation. Grandfathering is a role different than fathering, which my role model defined as, "sit up straight, clean your room, and get a job." I followed the same pattern for years, until I used similar language with my granddaughter, and my son reminded me, "She's only four years old." Then I knew I had to change.

My new model was based on the Norwegian philosopher, Ivan the Terrible, who told me to just show up on time, watch their performance, cheering all the time, smile, and when they fell down, place them on your belly and rub their back while humming drinking songs. Bonus points are given if you get down on the floor and let them ride on your back, provided they don't exceed the posted weight limits.

Let me tell you a story about the power of the grandfather gift.

To pass the time on a long airplane flight, I was drawing elves and clowns. The woman, across the aisle watching me, told me that the daughter sitting next to her was also an artist. She introduced me to Emily, the larger of the two bundled up girls. Mom explained the reason for all Emily's Disney characters was that she and her daughters were on their way to Disneyland.

Just before we landed Emily finally spoke to me. "You look like the picture I have of my Grandpa. I never met him. He went to work and didn't come home. Right, Mommy?"

Mother nodded, and she mouthed the words, "9/11," while her daughter's head was turned. Then the Mom said to me, "Thank you for playing grandpa, even for a little while. I think taking the girls to Disneyland was something he might have done, so here we are. I wonder if we're not going for me as well."

I gave Emily my latest clown drawing, and signed it "to a special girl." She rewarded me with a wide smile. I couldn't speak; there were tears in my voice. It was early September 2009, with the pain and memories of 9/11, along with the healing power and privilege of being a borrowed grandfather. "Even for a little while."

I Hate to Exercise

I hate to exercise. I just bathe in sweat, get lightheaded, and reach a level of weariness unnatural for a man of my age. Yet, I do go to the gym at least four days, sometimes five days a week. Why, a reasonable person might ask. Fear, on the verge of terror! I am not afraid of dying. I just don't want to go until I have seen all the new series on Netflix. Plus, there are examples of too many late friends who said, "Don't worry, there is a pill for that." May they rest in peace.

The gym, in the early hours between six and eight AM, is where I meet My People. At this time, there is a mix of working people and retired folks who are unable to sleep late. The latter either go to bed with the sun, or else during the night, they count trips to the bathroom instead of sheep. At the gym, I learn the score of last night's ballgame, the name of the craftsman who will fix my roof—at a reasonable price, and the state of the economy. In between I exercise, somehow managing to fit a 60-minute workout into two hours. This special learning continues in the locker room, my personal Wikipedia.

At the same gym, there are serious athletes, who actually run on a treadmill, move the cross trainer so fast they are a blur, and lift the weight of two sixteen-year old grandsons. These women are not my people! My people walk, then talk. My people lift, then rest. My people do an hour of yoga, then need coffee, a doughnut, and a nap.

We exercise not for hard bodies, or to impress. We exercise, because we want to maintain the ability to get out of a chair without using our arms. We stretch and bend, so that we can garden and play golf. We walk, so we can keep our freedom to go anywhere we want to go. We lift weights, so we can lift a grandchild, and hold him or her in our arms. We do our best with what we have left, which is more than enough.

We all know as we age, exercise is very important to our health and self-esteem. My doctor encouraged me to exercise. What keeps me coming back, in addition to the above benefits, is the image of a man with an artificial leg who was walking faster than me on a treadmill, or the woman on chemotherapy who exercised, despite the side effects of the treatment. Someday, I hope to be good enough to be one of Their People. Someday... Until then, I hear a nap calling so I can store up enough energy to come back tomorrow.

A Codgerism: When I smile, no one will recognize me in disguise. When I laugh, they join, and forget I am an old guy.

The Artist Within

Despite failing eyesight and a lack of natural talent, I signed up for a drawing class. It was held in a dank basement. Water ran down one wall into a loud sump pump in a corner. It was offered during daylight hours, when the light was stronger, not to mention, free. My companions were a cast of characters worthy of at least a year of serious study. They were six older women and a twenty-something woman who was legally blind. Really, in a drawing class. She was not bad, really! IT'S TRUE! YOU JUST CAN'T MAKE THIS STUFF UP!

Two of the women wore hearing aids, frequently left at home, which caused the instructor to shout, so that by the end of the session, she sounded like a pregnant frog. One of the hearing-challenged women claimed she could pick up FM radio on her device. She would give traffic updates and weather reports, or tap her pencil in time to classical music. The other got lost every week, so she arrived fifteen to thirty minutes late. At the end of class, one of us walked her to the parking lot to help her find her car. One week we noticed a man in the lot idling his car. She had forgotten her husband was picking her up. Another classmate loudly announced she had an appointment, and left for the day when she did not like the lesson.

The young woman with vision difficulties was able to see outlines. She could draw if she placed her face close to the paper. Since we were drawing with pencil, by the end of class, the tip of her nose was smudged black, as if she had played noses with a chimney sweep. She had a driver's license, and drove a huge white truck with orange caution triangles on the doors and tailgate. A head-shaking experience! She was so nice I was sure if she hit someone, she would take him home for dinner.

The last two women were without blemish, therefore not worth talking about, except to say I never saw anyone wear dresses, heels, and hats suitable for an Easter Parade to an art class. Unlike the others, they were not my people.

I worked hours drawing furniture, landscapes, fruit bowls, and a few objects still to be identified, in order to bring home my efforts to Sweets, like a dog with a prize bone. Each week she would say something like, "Interesting, h-m-m. What is it?" Sweets, a highly intelligent woman, was unable to understand the artist within.

At the end of the course, I took my efforts for a second opinion, to Franco, who owns an art gallery near the dump. He leaned over, looked closely, stood back, held one bent arm by the elbow. Then spun around, looked me in the eye, and said, "Don't Quit Your Day Job!" I told him I was retired, but valued his opinion. "I hear they're hiring greeters with your skills at Walmart," he said with a sneer. Too late! I have already signed up for metal sculpture class this summer with my new friends. We get to use a welding torch. Wow!!

Your Name Is ???

Sweet Nancy and I have ten children, but none from our own marriage. My son is married to Sweet's daughter, and it is legal in every state. The word unique is an understatement. We had so many different names on our mailbox in New Jersey, that whenever the mailman was confused by a name, the letter ended up in our box. In other families we might be called Mom and Dad; in our family the children called us The Parents, which was synonymous with opponent or oppressor.

Mealtimes were always loud and unruly. I, in an attempt to restore order, would rebuke the offending youngster by name, The Wrong Name! Sometimes I would go though two or three names or more before hitting the jackpot. The delay provided a brief amusement for all, including my wife. I wonder if those times were the source of my high blood pressure.

Recently one of my sons, who had been dating a woman with a mere two children, wondered out loud in amazement, "How did you ever put up with me?" He must have forgotten the times I took him into the woods and left him there. His mother would tie bright ribbons to trees so he could find his way home. My wife doesn't remember any of this and accuses me of telling Irish stories. Hah!

I still have difficulty remembering people's names, even though I see them frequently, but at least we are not related. There are people from my church that I see every Sunday, as well as people in my gym, whom I see four or five days a week, not to mention my neighbors, who I see every day. In order to save them embarrassment, I call all the guys Bud and the women Darlin', a trick I learned in Alabama. Usually I remember the missing name as soon as we part. Then there is this woman who sits across from me at mealtimes. I know that I know her name; but somehow I keep losing the honey-do list she leaves for me. There are days when not remembering is a gift acquired through years of practice.

Have a good day, Despite The Odds! Remember your grandchildren will love you no matter what happens. If you don't have grandchildren, rent one.

Christmas Gifts

Each year, despite my leaving post-it notes all over the house, the Sweet One tells me she never knows what I need for Christmas, my birthday, St. Patrick's Day, the day I first became a grandfather, etc. When I whine about her ignoring my stack of notes she replies, "They're just guy toys, not what you really Need."

In the interest of peace, harmony, and survival, I offer the following of what a gentleman in his autumn years may need:

- A gyroscope attached to his belt that will keep him on the level when he loses his balance.
- A hearing aid that serves as an MP3 player when visiting difficult relatives that automatically gives updates of either the Red Sox or the Patriot games.
- A pocket device that disables all cell phones in a fifteen foot area around the mature gentleman.
- A voice recognition system hidden in your glasses that is activated when someone says hello. It then prints out their name on the inside of your glasses.
- A memory chip that text messages the reason you are standing in your cellar, attic or bathroom. Activate by humming to yourself.
- Button that states, "Unless you are mentioned in the will, please call me Mr. Codger not by my front name.
- Glasses that first glow in the light or in the dark, and if not touched for five minutes, begin to say, "Here I am," over and over.
- A screen in the remote that reminds him of birthdays, his anniversary, his best friend's name, and instructions his wife may leave when she is out of town.

All of the above may be purchased by CODGERS R US, where their motto is, "If you lost it, give us enough money, we will find it. Cash only." I.M. Lost, Mgr.

If the truth be told, I really don't need any Thing. I am at the time of my life that what I treasure most are good friends, a call from my family, a funny story, hugs from my grandchildren, homemade ice cream and the love of my good wife. I wouldn't turn down a ride in the backseat of a Rolls Royce one leaf-filled October Day.

Now where did I put my car keys to the old sedan?

Grandpa's Confusion

Hello grandchildren, this is your confused, old grandpa writing in the old time way, with pen and paper. I do remember you asked me to communicate with you on something called Facebook. I did try it once, but it was full of pictures with very little writing. I have too many wrinkles to put this face in a book that goes who knows where. Besides, I keep forgetting my password. I don't want to be your "friend." I just want to be your grandpa. So I am writing you to ask for help in order to clear up some confusion I have about your world. I feel like I'm living in a foreign country.

Remember, I still drive in good and bad weather. It seems everywhere I travel, I see you young people wearing hooded shirts, talking to their hand. I drive on our college campus in good weather and watch students talking to their hand, and walk into other people, or onto the street with its oncoming traffic. In bad weather they walk in the pouring rain, without a raincoat or an umbrella, still talking to their hand. What is happening here? Please, tell me that you own an umbrella. I worry. Ask your Grandmother.

Then there is something called texting, practiced by young people with large thumbs. Mimi and I went out to dinner and watched a young couple on a date, sitting a few tables away, staring into their laps, and rapidly moving their thumbs. When I asked the waiter, he smiled and said they were texting. Is this a substitute for sex, something you can do in public? Honey, take some advice from your grandfather, I don't care how big your thumbs get, it can't be as much fun. Don't you believe it! Although, it would eliminate a lot of unwanted pregnancies, I suppose. I am sending this in the spring, so you will probably receive it in the summer, considering the financial condition of the post office.

During a hot summer, Mimi and I like to find a cool lake. When we got out of the car the last time, I asked Mimi if she brought my thongs. A group of teen-age girls standing nearby, all roared in laughter, fell to the ground with tears in their eyes, and pointed at me. "Do you hear what he said?" one asked through her tears. When they stopped laughing, one young gal explained to me that a thong was a type of woman's underwear. I asked, "How can any woman wear a sandal with rubberized ropes as underwear? Doesn't it hurt, and how do you keep warm in winter?" They screamed in laughter and ran off.

Grandchildren, I need help. Now I am being laughed at. I am really confused. Perhaps you could come over for dinner and explain this new world. Mimi will make your favorite meal, all homemade, with one of her special pies. Send me an e-mail with the days you could be available. You still use e-mail don't you? Make it soon, we are thinking of taking a backpacking trip in the Grand Canyon, or was it the Green Mountains? I forget. Mimi has a GSP, GPU or something like that, so I'm sure we will find our way.

Love, Mimi and Boppa

(SENT FROM THE FAVORITE
GRANDDAUGHTER'S SMART PHONE)

Hi, Grandpa T,

Thanks for your recent letter. I have never received a letter written in red ink before; it reminded me of my elementary school English teacher's notes. I did have to ask Mimi to help me understand certain words. If you decide to use a computer again, Spell Check is wonderful for so many people; I can't write without it. Mimi says you write like an overworked doctor, whatever that means. Since she worked as a nurse, she must know something about doctors.

Grandpa, we are worried about you. How ever are you going to deal with our world? Even Mom uses you as a bad example. Whenever we kids are too lazy to study, Mom says something like, "If you don't put the time in to learn new skills, you will end up like your grandfather." Maybe if you tried a little harder…

I just don't understand how someone like you, who uses a Kindle to enlarge the letters to read books, owns a laptop, takes walks with your iPod Touch, so you can listen to your music, and check sports scores and the stock market, is so out of touch. Grandpa, you have to learn more than how to turn these things on and off. You have to accept there are no manuals to hold in your hand. They are online or buried in the device. Grandpa, it's a wonderful world, open the door. We will help you when we come for dinner.

Dad doesn't want me to drive with you anymore. He freaks out because you have two GPSs that you use at the same time. He thinks it's insane that you ignore both of them, and instead, ask Mimi or one of us grandkids to give you directions from a map. I tried to tell him that you trust us more than "any stinking machine," but he just walks out of the room mumbling in a foreign language. Personally, I like telling an adult where to go!

Your Geek grandson will be texting you, or if you are lucky, will send an e-mail to explain about smart phones and texting. Don't worry; I do have an umbrella. It makes a great door stopper when I need to be alone in my room.

Did you get my thank you letter? The money will really help with school expenses.

ILU, which is texting for I love you.

Approved by Codger Tom and Sweets

Dear Special Granddaughter,

As you suggested, I am reluctantly writing to you on my computer so that I can use Spell Check, or since I own a Mac, is it called iCheck? I have a few last questions on how your world operates.

I recently saw a chart in a real newspaper that indicated people, under the age of twenty, must plug into an electronic device every 30 minutes, those under thirty, every 45 minutes. It takes my people two days for us just to find the power button. My question is, what happens when we have one of our New England storms, and we lose power for days? Are young people prone to become violent with a delayed electronic encounter? Do I need protection? I know you will find it unbelievable that one week I forgot to check my e-mail, and another time, I lost my phone until Grandma found it holding a door open.

You are starting college now, the second wave of our grandchildren to do so. The last wave found their life mates during that time. I have been wondering if you will do the same. This leads to my second question; what is speed internet dating, and does that interest you enough to try? Two college students at our gym were discussing one young man's experience. As I understand it, you send in your name, location, and photo, and then post it online. If a female responds, you have two minutes or less to convince her to date you. If she accepts, you send her a virtual drink, and voilá, you have a date. The student had ten dates in one night. I wondered what a virtual drink tasted like? At the end, do you kiss your smart phone goodnight? I may be old, but I think you are missing something! I am so confused, perhaps you could explain how young people find someone to love with this method.

I may be confused, because when I dated a girl, it took me ten minutes to sputter my name, family background, employment history, and show proof of my tetanus shots. It then took another two hours to convince her father that I was not Albert, the axe murderer, and despite malicious rumors, my intentions were honorable, mostly.

I recently heard of a dating service for older people that requires them to show up in living color to meet the other person. This is necessary, because of a widely held distrust due to Photoshop. Prior to such a meeting, you must submit a list of your medications, previous open-heart surgeries, bionic limbs, and emergency numbers. Plus it asks whether you drive at night. They have real drinks such as coffee, tea, or twenty-year old Scotch.

When you get to college, write to me, so that I know you are doing all right. Mention to your father, known in his younger days as Crash, that if he is still thinks of banning you from taking trips with me, I have the photos where he is standing next to his car with rollover dents in the roof. Only one click away from YouTube!

Love to the family,

Grandpa T, alias Codger Tom, with Sweet Grandma, editor and censor.

The Little Librarian

I have always loved librarians. Probably because a librarian with a page-boy haircut, tweed skirt, tan sweater, and sensible shoes allowed me, a fifth grader, into the adult section to read, but not to take out books. The adult section was a sanctuary for a shy boy, and opened the world of adventure, mystery, and I hoped, hidden knowledge that would give me confidence. My hope was that I, a small boy, could grow tall on a diet of large books.

A father wished to pass his love of reading to his son, John, and he may also have wished to enlarge his son's world. But John had little interest in books; however, he loved to build things out of wood. So he eagerly agreed to his dad's idea to build a little house.

A neighbor had just finished building a deck, so there was an abundance of free building material. The floor and ceiling were made from a bike ramp. There are little glass doors that open in the front of the house. Dad did the sawing; John hammered and painted. John's sister helped paint the final coat. The grandparents donated shutters. When it was finished, Dad sent in an application and the $20 fee to become the first little Free Library in Fairhope, Alabama. They secured the house to a post, and dug a hole at the end of the driveway. They filled it with books and opened a neighborhood library. It contains both children and adult books, free for all. A small sign below the house reads, "Take a book, leave a book."

This family is part of a worldwide movement that promotes access to reading. Dad says it's working; his son is reading more. The Little Free Library has a small comment book, written in by people from three southern states, plus

Minnesota, Wisconsin, and Toronto, Canada. "Great idea, you give me hope that we will read books that you hold in your hands." "I can walk to your library, so thank y'all."

A tall, young woman walking her dog stopped, turned to me, and asked if she could leave books, as she was traveling and "Jost loved the idea." Since the Little Free Library has branches all over the world, I suggested perhaps she could donate in her country. She looked down and said, "I am from Bulgaria; such things do not exist in my country." Then she smiled and asked if I had heard of something they did have in her country, Books Across Borders.

Books Across Borders was started in countries devastated by wars that destroyed most of the publishing houses. If you owned a book you thought others should read, you registered it on their website, and received a tracking device which you affixed to the book. The book was then left in a public place like a coffee house, tavern, or outdoor cafe for someone to read. The book-giver logged onto the website so that he or she could learn where the book went.

She said, "I have books that have traveled all over Europe and Canada. Today I will leave books in your country."

In a world where we seem so divided, there are still places with enough light to see how we can come together. Let us celebrate dads who pass on the love of reading to their sons.

May all the dads out there have a Happy Father's Day.

Cookies at Funerals

I go to funerals, like my father did before me; recently, two in a single week. I like the triangle sandwiches and the cookies. In my father's time the cookies were home made, and respected women made their signature cakes. I still remember my mother made her coveted dark chocolate cake with buttercream icing when my father died. She showed her love with her hands. She made her best, because it was a time when words felt empty, and she needed to do something, anything, anything to smooth the raw edges of her loss.

In my mile square town, a death was a tolling for the community. Men washed and polished their long black cars, getting ready for the procession of family and close friends from church to grave children were expected to run countless errands carrying goods and information. But mostly they were called into service to watch the youngest, while mommas and daughters made huge casseroles, warm and full of comfort smells and caring. This coming together of the many, eased the burden of the few, sitting in hard chairs with aching hearts.

In my home, when I was young and someone was sick or dying, I would be sent outside to play. On one such day, I found Skinny Kenny, the fastest kid in town. Kenny didn't have many friends; his family owned the local funeral home. Kids thought he was a bit creepy. They could have been right; we often played hide and seek in the coffins.

One day, Kenny shushed me, and told me to hide after he crawled inside and I closed the lid. When two workmen came to get the coffin, Kenny sat up and moaned. We didn't know adults could run that fast. I have since given up my irreverent childish ways. There have been far too many losses.

During my Dad days, I learned that children left in the dark fill the empty spaces with sleepless nights. I gave my children the information they needed to face the hard edges in life. My own father and I did not spend much time together. He worked long hours managing a store; his customers often became his friends. He introduced me to cranky old men and heavily perfumed women. He told me about their gifts, or how important they were to their family. He shared their moments of success, and how they overcame difficulty. Looking at these people, I began to doubt my father's sanity. He always went to their funerals, and he forced me to go, too. I hated those funerals full of incense and sadness.

These many years later, I find myself going to funerals, seeing those rascally men who have left our men's group through the eyes of their families' love. It's a reluctant inheritance my Dad gave me so long ago. I was too young to understand. It's taken me all these years, to begin to fit into his large shoes.

The Strawberry Children

"Say Mister, have you got a long minute? I am an old man with a short story that needs telling before the Lord calls me home. I come from a place you Yankees call the panhandle of Florida. Since I have been retired all these years, I now live in Plant City, the Strawberry Capital of the World. I was raised and will probably die near the strawberries.

"Ever hear about the Strawberry Children? Probably not, to most folks we were invisible. The growers would hire whole families to pick. We would pick from sunrise till dark, six days a week, from January through March. We didn't go to school for three months, making the time up in the summertime. Ever been to Florida in summer? You get used to it, mostly. Kids would see us in the field on the way to school, and thinking we were immigrants, made fun of us, and named us Strawberry Children. But I tell you, I could pick like a grown man, one hundred pounds a day. My back needed that Sunday off. We learned to work hard then, and for the rest of our life-long lives. Sundays we lived like a big family; everybody would bring food. Someone would have a fiddle, and we'd dance until we wuz silly.

"Daddy went to college for two years, but they needed him at home. So he became a farmer. He loved to farm, but I never took to it. He loved us hard, and wanted us to go to school to be somebody. Maybe that's why something broke between us when I didn't take to books, and nagged him until he signed the papers so I could join the Marines. I learned in the Marines that you didn't have to die to go to hell; you could do that at Paris Island. Still, if the marines didn't get hold of me, I'd be dead now, like my brother. They taught me how to fix machines so I had a trade.

"I was lucky; I came home in one piece, got a factory job, married, and had me some children. I saved some money and started to wonder where all those vacation trailers were going to park. So I took my money, put another mortgage on the house, and bought some land. I opened the second trailer park in the state of Florida. The whole family helped run it, 'cause I kept my job as maintenance foreman working at night. We did all right, and when I sold it a few years back, I could retire and do some traveling. Last year the wife and I went to China. That sure wuz something to see.

"I'm flying with you to see my son and grandson; they're both ministers in Montana. I'm just an old man now, but my children make me so proud. So Mister, maybe you could let a few people know about the Strawberry Children, who grew up, served in the war, paid their taxes, and put food on your table. You know sometimes when I eat a strawberry, as crazy as it sounds, far off, I swear I can still hear that fiddle. I wonder what happened to those other children."

I kept my promise, Calvin, now a few people know your story.

The Season of Giving Thanks

She was a lady from Virginia, he a rough, redheaded Irishman from Boston. Her mother claimed she would *just die*, if she married that man, and a Yankee besides. This made him so much more desirable for the young girl. His mother wanted a priest in the family, so any woman would be a disappointment.

Friends claimed the marriage was doomed without a family blessing. It was, therefore, a wonder to all when, sixty years later, they celebrated their wedding anniversary. Their four children would tell stories how they both saw the world through different lenses, how every year they cancelled each other's vote, and they went to plays, movies, and book clubs in order to argue all the way home. Their relationship growing deeper gave hope to many.

Every morning, after coffee, he reads her the newspaper. She still loves the color words take on listening to his deep brogue, for now she sees only shapes. He brings her books for the blind and is rewarded with a giggle and a warm smile. From her wheelchair she tells him how to work the stove and the washing machine. In winter, he wraps her in sheets warmed in the dryer, to ease the stiffness of arthritis. They put on an old tune, dance in place, remembering the early years.

When his memory stumbles, and no one calls for advice or direction, she teases him without mercy, helping him remember when he served in a great army that kept a whole nation from harm. Does he want to try on his old uniform to see if it fit? She smiles as she remembered his gentle hand in growing the children, and didn't they just turn out fine. She reminds him he gave our grandchildren caring daddies, and they so love their Pepaw. It always surprises him how she is able is able to light up all his dark places, filling him with her laughter.

This man is one of an army of such men, without natural skills or experience, who have taken the awkward steps to care for someone who had spent a good time of her life caring for us. By nature men want to fix, move on, not feel so helpless when someone we love suffers so. At one time, many years ago, their story was my story.

Men may shout about politics, the stupidity of baseball umpires, or the sorry state of the economy, but we seldom tell you how it was to take care of a wife broken by disease or injury. If pressed, they will tell you without detail, "It was the right thing to do." You may know such a man as brother, friend, or husband. I know them as Bruce, Bill, and Bob. Then there is Don, John, Vern, and Leon, to name a few. They have shared their stories with me, and on this November day, I thank them for that privilege. You are the men who have allowed another to lean on you, and you were there.

Television Makes You Fat

After hours of research using Netflix as my baseline, I have concluded that television has the same strange power over me that Celine Barbarosa had when I was fourteen. Whenever she came within ten feet of me, bathed in exotic perfume, wearing pink shorts and a halter top, my brain turned to silly putty.

I had, until the last few months, been able to restrict my viewing to a movie or two a week, with occasional expanded viewing during weather emergencies. No longer! I think it started when we sought a divorce from our old television set after eighteen years of use, and purchased a high definition, large screen TV, so we could read subtitles on British mysteries. I rediscovered football when I realized the ant people on the field were actually players. Then one day Sweets discovered the joy of binge watching, or series chugging, when she brought home the complete seasons of "The Good Wife," "House of Cards," and "Judge, John Deed."

Soon after I met a family at Hubert's, a local clothing store, purchasing extra-huge sweat-suits solely for watching television. The previous weekend they had watched twenty-two episodes of "Breaking Bad." Their eyes still were glazed, and their lips were puffy in a rainbow of colors, evidence of snack overdose. It was pitiful; and rather than stopping the addiction, they were buying larger, less revealing clothing.

It was at that time I began to wonder, could our problem with obesity be a result of television? In my own case, I had blamed Sweets for my tight pants. Did she dry my pants at high heat too long? Were manufacturers using inferior material, subject to shrinkage, forgetting the magazine article that pointed out the US has the dubious distinction of watching more television than anyone else in the world, five hours for each resident. Have you noticed there aren't any commercials for broccoli, carrots, or skim milk? Thank God, or else our wives would have more ammunition to lead to the path of healthy, tasteless living.

I am writing this essay during the week leading up to Super Bowl Sunday, when we will eat 14,500 tons of potato chips, and 1.23 billion chicken wings. Remember the chicken wing shortage crisis one recent year? Super Bowl Sunday has been touted as the largest combination sports-party event of the year. One source claims we spend fifty billion dollars over a four-day period for this one event. The modern version of a Roman Orgy!

Since my fall from clean, pure living due to television, I thought I would fully participate in our culture's decadent living; I asked Sweets to get me for my February birthday a power assisted recliner with back massage. It featured Butt Kicker bass speakers in the seat, dual lighted cup holders, snack trays stored in the chair arms, and was outlined with ambient lighting for safe returns from bathroom trips. "You have not lived long enough, or been dead long enough for something like that. How about I buy you a bean bag chair with the Patriots' logo?" Reality has a way of invading the sweetest dreams.

It's time to hide the remote and pull the plug. There's a new television world streaming into our homes, easier to access, and harder to resist. It tells us to have Bud with our friends, a Papa John's family size pizza, an order of a five-gallon tub of chicken wings, and incidentally, increase our health care policy. I have met the enemy, and it is my TV.

Just Say the Words

Wednesday was the day I visited Howard—every week between 11 AM and noon. Each day he touched on his favorite subject, women. They were his girls, and the women who cared for him in the assisted living center. His girls were his adult daughters who had families of their own. His daughters washed his clothes, paid his bills, called or visited daily, and harassed him to get well when he wanted to give up.

He told me, "Now that I'm ninety-four and my wife is deceased, they give me the love they learned from their mother. I'm blessed twice."

"Did you ever tell them how you appreciate all their love and attention?" I asked as I walked with him to the dining room.

"Well, I took care of them, besides, they know."

I replied, "Not if you never told them."

Somewhere as you read this, there is a woman who is so busy she eats her lunch standing, yet takes time to phone you between work, errands, and cooking in order to say, "Hi Dad, how are you?" Then she waits and listens when you respond. She is a woman, who like her own mother, locks herself in the bathroom to steal five minutes of privacy, yet who breaks down your walls of silence with a hug. She is your daughter, or in my case, my stepdaughter.

Some daughters grew up taking care of resistant brothers, stray cats, and running errands for the elderly neighbor. A type of junior mother of the family. Other daughters were the wild child, locking swords with mother. She grew into the role when she had her own children. This is the daughter who regularly calls and has long phone conversations with her former enemy.

There are even a few who learned directly from the teachings of her mother. Whatever the path was, the gift as well as the responsibility, was passed to the next generation. So it goes, as we watch our granddaughters inherit the skills for family unity.

My old friend, Howard, is gone now, but not the lessons he taught me. I miss him. This year in addition to honoring my wife, I plan to make a phone call to Montana, to our daughter, the Guardian of the Sacred Grandchildren. I will then awkwardly, for it does not come naturally to me, tell her how by having her in my life, I am twice blessed with her as my daughter, and what a fine mother she has become to the grandchildren.

I am sure there is a roomful of daughters, in addition to my own, who have been waiting their whole lives for your own words that say, "I am so glad you are my daughter, and my life has been made richer by your love. Thank you."

Happy Mothers Day!!!

Small Town Christmas

Christmas celebrations are done differently in small towns. I grew up in a small New Jersey town, Sweet Nancy in Wisconsin. We both counted the days until those towns became a small memory in our rear view mirror. Years later with children grown and carving their own path, we have returned to our roots. Like a marriage, we have learned through the years to love the people and the geography of life in our New England town.

Back in the day, Christmas season began the day the Sears Roebuck catalog arrived in the mail. Three inches thick, it weighed around 5 lbs. It would soon disappear into a dark corner or under a child's bed for days, only to reappear and be fought over again. When Sweets and I were young, we shopped locally, and the shopkeepers not only knew your name, but also your teacher's first name. Today we browse the internet for ideas, and shop in town whenever possible. The shop owners are our neighbors, and in summer they sponsor concerts on the town green.

In my mile square town of childhood, Santa came to town via Main Street, riding a fire engine with its lights flashing and siren screaming, as small children hid under their mother's coat for protection. Firemen threw candy while Santa drove out of town to the North Pole.

Here, Santa comes to our welcome center, riding in a farm wagon, dressed in a plaid woolen coat and wearing L.L. Bean boots. He sits in a shed while children climb into his lap to tell him their dream list. Wood elves designed by well-known children's author, Tomie dePaola, dot the snow. Tomie lives on the other side of town; once Sweets compared tomatoes in the supermarket with him. There's a high school choir caroling in the season. We see some of the young people in our church. The bank across from the library offers doughnuts and hot chocolate. It's small town nice; we get to talk to the neighbors before the snow keeps us inside by the fire.

That white church in the middle of town owns an important slice of our country's history, a Revere bell. I've climbed to the top of the steeple to see it. The view of our bell and the town is impressive; so are all the church choirs this holiday season. It's Christmas; people fill the pews. Parents will see their kid's teachers in the choir, and probably the owner of the local paper will usher you to a seat. The houses of worship all leave their doors open; it's a birthday party, everyone is invited.

Life has come full circle. On our early path we had ambition. We aimed for independence as we sought our fortune, working to prove ourselves, to have our own family, where we would do things right. In life, we may have to go away to find our calling. But there comes a time when we want to be in community, and do all the things we never had time for before. And perhaps discover a talent for doing something we never knew existed. It's Christmas time, when we all seek to go home. It not just a small town; it's the end of our journey; we have found our home.

THOMAS DONNELLY

Get Out the Glue, Honey,
I'm Falling Apart

The tall distinguished-looking man sidled up to me in the lobby of the concert hall. He said in a low voice, "Eh, Buddy, rotator cuff?" His black sling looked sleek and supple. "Yes," I answered, trying to hide my dull gray sling with an immobilizer the size of a cement block strapped to my waist.

Over the course of the next five weeks, strange men and women told me they had been, at one time, part of the Union of RC Survivors. Guys would chortle uproariously and shout, "How're you doing with toilet paper?" They looked disappointed when informed that my good arm was fine, so toilet paper wasn't an issue. Women would smile sympathetically and tell me, "It could have been worse; you could have died; and besides, your wife was a nurse. "

How many of you reading this have had the experience of one day being a normal human, and a short time later, someone was tying your shoes, monitoring your medications, driving you to a place where people in white coats probed and looked through machines into secret places in your body? Have you had friends who said, "How are we feeling today?" or "You look good," in much the same way one talks about a body at a wake.

Most confusing were the people who would punch me in the arm with the sling, or grab my sore shoulder and ask," So, how's it going?" Didn't they see I was wounded? It was at these times I'd want to shout to Sweet Nancy, "Get out the glue, Honey, I'm falling apart," followed by going to my bedroom and slamming the world outside.

It is at these times you find your true friends: Those folks who call just to listen, drop off a meal, tell you a bad joke, or who tell you they miss you, and are counting the days until you are well again. Then there are those special people who bring the wine and cheese, listen to you whine how life is unfair, and make you laugh as you fall apart.

Critter Wars

It has been a long New Hampshire winter, too long. I am writing this at the end of April, and it is snowing. I just know that somewhere there is Spring, but not here. Even the native born New Englanders are snarling and shaking their fist at the sky, crying "Enough!" However, New London historian, thespian, and poet, Lloyd Littlefield, just sent me an e-mail describing the event as a "winter wonderland." I wonder if poets hear whimpers, cries, and the gnashing of teeth as raw material for their art?

Perhaps my mood has been influenced by the invasion! We went on vacation, and upon our return discovered that Mickey Mouse and his undocumented relatives had moved in. The mouse thugs had trashed our kitchen, throwing wild parties, eating EVERYTHING they could get their paws on, and throwing the wrappers in the air, as evidenced by the trail of mouse manure marking their path of destruction. They even made a nest in the back of a sofa cushion!

Sweet Nancy, who leaves the room if there is a whisper of violence on a TV show, went into the bathroom, changed her clothes, and became Nan the Avenger. (drum roll please) She quickly set traps, put out poison, and set up the unlicensed force of maximal destruction, the Wisconsin Death Ray. Within days mouse bodies stacked up like cordwood! Sweets lives by the motto, "You can play in my attic, but touch my kitchen, and you are grave yard dead." Speaking of cold and dead, did I mention it was still snowing?

Through the years, we have lost animal battles to gluttonous squirrels at bird feeders, plant ravaging deer, raccoon raids on the very night the corn ripens, and bears that carry off bear proof garbage cans for a midnight snack. All this we have endured. These are the times when God's critters step on my last remaining nerve ending. Crank up the dial on the Death Ray, this is war and it's still snowing!

Death Ray for rent.

Notes From a Wrinkled Valentine

Our New England heating systems are wonderful sound conductors. Sitting next to a heat duct, I am often entertained, as I listen to meetings in another part of the building. Doing this, I have noticed when two or more women gather, a competition develops to see who is married to the man with the most character defects. This includes a general consensus about men in general, and their crimes against humanity and common sense. They mention offenses such as leaving the toilet seat up, or not filling the empty gas tank, or forgetting to tell her about the party being held tonight for her mother's second husband's brother. Worst is their inability to remember details, like his sister breaking her arm when she totaled her snowmobile, or what foods were served at his cousin's funeral, or the results of his secret doctor's visit. Little details that make life interesting.

In most of my professional life I have worked closely with intelligent, articulate, witty women and heard the same complaints. I wonder if this type of talk promotes connection and is an entry into more intimate conversation. When I have asked women why they stay in the marriage if hubby is so bad, they laugh, "Sometimes I wonder." Then they say something like this, "You need to lighten up, we're just venting. We complain, but then go home and make dinner. We're not leaving, and compared to others, my guy is not so bad. We have been together a long time."

It may be that only when we have enough couple history can we become really comfortable with that person sharing our lives. Perhaps most of us are like other seasoned couples who have developed an ease with each other, by walking through walls of misunderstanding, looking for a door to open during long hours of troubled talk. We have moved beyond stealing blankets during the night to waiting long hours in medical offices, holding our breath. We, the survivors of heated battles with strong-willed children, can now enjoy the fruits of our labor—grandchildren! We have developed a resolve that whatever comes, in each and every turn of the road, we will be together. (Except for occasional bathroom breaks.) Some couples that stay together for decades have developed a reverse paranoia, which is, our partners are here to do us good. This may serve to build a better life.

Now in the winter of their lives, she may smile and call him an old fool. He may complain about her fussing. They have done this for years. It is simply their dance. If she were to stop fussing and he wasn't such a challenge, they would miss it and then what would they talk about?

It's the long, cold-filled nights of February; a time for hot chocolate and shared blankets with your valentine. Remind each other of the day when you first met, talk not only of how far you have traveled together, but the surprises awaiting you in the future.

Hibernating Among the Cobwebs

When the hard frost touches the ground in morning light, and darkness visits earlier each day, I go underground among the cobwebs of winter, to be softened by a blanket of warmth from the woodstove. Something within well-seasoned men finds sweet comfort in creating sawdust amid the sounds of an oldies station broadcasting from the paint splattered radio, sitting on the shelf you made with your son so long ago.

I come from a people who believe a cellar is a place for storing potatoes, onions, apples, old paint, tires, and twenty years of National Geographic. I have heard of people who have basement gyms, rec rooms, and wine cellars, and wonder what their lives are like without a winter retreat. I had an uncle who spent an entire happy day, ankle deep in sawdust, unaware of a raging snowstorm in the outside world. Aunt Edna was not pleased. I wonder if a cobweb filled cellar is a room made just for men.

Sweets prefers the sunlight, and seldom makes her way down the stairs. When she does, she comes armed with a spray can of air freshener in one hand and a broom in the other, humming chants she heard an old monk use while going into the catacombs. Years ago, she came down one day to tidy up. I couldn't find my tools that I needed for home repair for months, so therefore I was forced to rest until I finally found them. We now have an understanding.

When it's chilly, I do my best thinking in my rocking chair, staring at the fire in the stove. Thinking is hard work at my age, and sometimes I have been known to close my eyes for a spell. Recently after a strenuous afternoon in my thinking position, I pondered the following thought's. Is having a corner of our own an ancient need? For some it's a section of a garage where they can hammer and bend. For others it's an old desk in the attic, where they take time to collect thoughts and write them down. There are others who spend the winter planning a dooryard garden, because hands in the dirt feed their soul. I knew a guy who had an ice-house in the middle of a frozen lake; there he caught up on his reading until spring came and the ice melted. One mother I knew had a sewing room, so she could lock the door and be away from the endless needs of children. There she found the edges that she had known before the children came along.

Could this be the reason for winter, when forced by short days, cold winds, and ice to hunker down, so we can take time to find our edges of who we are, what we need, and what makes us truly happy? It's a thought worth pondering this winter.

Grady and the Guys

Many gray-haired guys grew up working on cars, loving the smell of new tires as much as we loved the smell of bread baking in the oven. Throw in a little oil, and we are on an express trip to a time when we had more hair, and we could tune a motor without a computer. A time when "hot" meant a fast car, not a sexy woman.

One year, while running away from winter to Alabama, I needed a set of tires. Enter Fairhope Tire and a world of special guys. The calendar on the showroom wall said, "We have two seasons, hunting and fishing." Max, the resident dog, sniffed me, grew bored, and moved on to stalk more exciting game. Behind the counter a small boy bounced around in a red car walker. He owned a long name, Grady Thrasher Blake, and a wide smile. His daddy, Geoff, wearing a grown-up version of that smile, welcomed me, and asked, "How can I help you?" I ordered the two tires he recommended.

I returned two days later when all the guys were eating. Geoff was feeding Grady, and since he was only ten months old, it was messy. On the other side of the table sat a mechanic and two tire changers eating fried chicken and biscuits, the Wednesday special. Grandma and co-owner, Rita Janson, buys the supplies for lunch (fried chicken, fish, soup, hot dogs, and hamburgers). Grandpa Ken, with Geoff's help, makes it. Not a helpless male in sight! If this wasn't enough to put a gold star over the door, it is what happened next that puts it head and shoulders above any usual business. Grandpa Ken started on my tire needs, then bounced Grady on his knee while talking on the phone. When a tire changer finished lunch, he picked up Grady, taking him to the rear of the showroom to play with

Max. When he had work to do, he turned the boy over to the other tire changer. Then the mechanic came from the back and took his turn, until finally Grady was placed back in the red racing car. The entire time, this much-loved little lad never touched the ground, but was held in the strong arms of caring men. Let me be perfectly clear, this is not an advertisement for Fairhope Tire. It is to me the finest example of men and business owners who care for families as much, if not more than, the bottom line. It gives me hope for the future.

Owners and grandparents, Rita and Ken, like other owners, set the tone for the business. They have owned Fairhope Tire since 1955, when they built the garage along with the organization. Hard work, family, and customer service still live here. As one of their customers told me, "Good people, good neighbors, a business with a heart. It is just a good place to buy tires." If you come early, you may be able to buy corn meal or grits, hand ground by Ken. When you look down behind the counter, a little guy in a red car will give you one of his smiles for free.

Come Back Visit:

On my return years later, Grady is six years old and in first grade. His little sister, Alora, age three, is in the care of grandmother, Rita, who has retired from the business. Mother, Amanda, is still working as a teacher, but Daddy, Geoff, has moved on to become a sales associate in another industry. Grandpa, Ken, has health concerns and is working toward retiring. Employee, grandson, Kyle, is learning how to ready the corn meal and grits from his grandpa, in order to carry on the tradition. Lunch is no longer provided, except on special occasions. Daughter, Julie, now runs the office, while the long-term mechanic handles the shop floor. The seeds Rita and Ken planted in 1955 continue to grow in this unique business, with the rare quality of serving the needs of customers without neglecting their family.

We feel privileged to share their story.

It's About Time

It's about time! A phrase often used to express the thought something is finally going to happen. When we were younger, our mothers used it when at last we focused our energy on school. Next, it marked the time we were able to stay up late; then the time we acquired a driver's license; graduated from high school and college; and after, time to find a job. The time came for us to marry and have children. All too soon, these same children spread their wings, and we thought about retiring and finally do what we wanted. I remember this as an awkward time. We had been parents and worked for so long. What do we talk about?

Thoughts of time have changed on this, the other side of the mountain. Some of us have begun to wonder, "How much time do I have left?" "What do I want to do?" "What experiences lie in the shadows, as yet undiscovered?" Sweets and I live by the motto, "We're older but bolder." Despite changes to our bodies, we find a way to open another door, often not knowing what the future holds.

Our daughter taught us to wear colors that make us look g-o-o-o-o-d! I have decided orange is my color, so I wear lots of it. I know that my choice is right, because when I am wearing orange, Sweets points to me, slaps her knee, and laughs so hard tears come to her eyes. Need I say more? Sweets is boldly writing her memoirs; I call them Mimi's Memories, a bawdy tale about growing up Lutheran in Wisconsin.

So if our children turn red with embarrassment, it's payback for all those phone calls from teachers and principals about their errant behavior. If you live long enough, payback is so sweet!

Stuff

Every day I carry on my person a pair of reading glasses, sunglasses, old guy coin container, pill container, pen, note pad with enclosed calculator, eye drops, Swiss army knife, and a novel to read while waiting for the next medical specialist. I am so tired of stuffing my pockets, looking like a penguin waddling through life. I need space.

I want a man bag like the English guys, because I have lots of stuff. I would style it in the American way. It would have a nylon strap to wear around the shoulder, with the working part in the shape of a gym bag, in a choice of guy colors, black, gray, or brown. We could cover it with the logos of our sports team or golf course—manly stuff.

Last year I purchased a Jumbo Wild Guy backpack with seventeen compartments and a hook on the outside for a water bottle, so I could pretend to be going somewhere. It worked so well my chiropractor says I should be able to stand up straight by Christmas. I began to wonder if I had a stuff problem, but wasn't having lots of stuff the American way? Sweets tells me I am the only guy she knows who goes to the dump with two bags and comes back with three. My grandson was mad at me because he wanted to watch baseball while I was watching American Picker, or was it Pawn Stars? I had to give him a bike that I just found on my last expedition to the dump, to buy his silence from Grandma.

So, I was ready to do something, when I noticed a poster on the wall in the food store.

"ARE YOU A PERSON WHO DRIVES A CAR WITH STUFF COVERING ALL THE SEATS EXCEPT YOUR

OWN? DO YOU HIDE YOUR STUFF IN THE ATTIC OR THE GARAGE, HOPING NO ONE WILL KNOW?"

Below in smaller letters, "We can help you shovel out from under the mound of STUFF and get your life back. STUFF ANONYMOUS."

The meeting was located in a place close enough to drive there, yet far enough so no one would know me. I would go after the sun goes down. That night I entered the room quietly, sat in the back row, and pulled a cap down over my face. I heard a woman had a seventeen-foot doublewide trailer in her back yard, just for her seasonal change of clothes. A man told of his collection of twenty-three Edsel automobiles, none of which were drivable.

"Gosh, I wasn't that bad; I didn't belong with these losers," I thought. I was just about to slip out the back door, when I felt a hand on my shoulder. All was lost! It was Louie, the neighborhood loudmouth.

"We wondered what was wrong with you. You were the only guy in the neighborhood who didn't have to mow his lawn, because you killed the grass with all your junk. We thought you sold ads for the local newspaper, since all your car seats were filled with papers; then the paper went online, and you still had the newspapers. How did you ever develop that walk like a penguin? My kids think it's cool. Welcome to SA, you're gonna love it. We can ride to meetings together. It will be fun, fun, fun!"

This may be worse than my double hernia surgery last summer. I'd move, but where would I put all my stuff?

Our Littlest Valentine

I remember the day early in my marriage when our lives changed forever. "Honey, I'm pregnant." I remember blurting, "How did that happen?" She let me know I was a willing participant in the process. Perhaps I should pay more attention to details. I gasped, "But I don't know how to be a dad." She answered, "Can't help you; I am going to have enough trouble being a mom." We said in unison, "Let's call our Moms; they'll know what to do, so the child will not die under our care."

We were parents of cloth diapers, held together with skin scarring safety pins. Diaper pails with fumes so harsh, they melted the paint off the walls. If we were blessed with home delivery diaper service for a month, we shouted with joy. With two months service, we'd name our next child after you. For us, caffeine was not a drug, but salvation. It enabled sleep deprived, incoherent parents to feed a starving child every two hours, 24/7. Think teen-agers on steroids. I have a picture of myself from this time, when I realized we would care for this little creature who cried non-stop for no apparent reason. Think deer in the headlights!

There is good reason for the confusion with the present generation. It starts with the news, "I am pregnant," changed into "We are pregnant." All this time I thought his round belly and humongous weight gain were due to beer and fear of exercise. They are the generation where nearly ninety per cent are connected to social media. Grandma's advice is fact checked, and knowledge comes from YouTube. Gone are the days of opening your wallet and showing a few pictures. Enter the ability to send two hundred internet pictures just the first week, starting with the delivery room. Some are streamed live from the crib using HD baby monitors. Because the web has no expiration date, years in the future, your grown child will give you the silent treatment for two years, because her bare bottom was seen by the wrong people.

The dads of yesterday were more involved in their bowling leagues than their children's lives, whereas today's dads get family leave to study the ancient art of connecting with a child using baby talk. That does limit conversations with former teammates and drinking buddies. Stay-at-home dads are more common. I wonder if dad-duties have become a major factor in the declining birth rate in the U.S.

This is the month when we celebrate Valentines Day; when we tell people we love how much they mean to us. Through the years our circle has enlarged to include grandchildren. Three times now the circle has pushed outward to include great-grandchildren. We did pretty well as grandparents. Great-grandparenting is still new. Recently, I awkwardly held my new great-granddaughter. There was a natural curve for her head resting on my shoulder. I patted her back, breathed in that smell of newness, and like snuggling kittens, was content in our small shadow of closeness. With each breath, I tasted again the miracle of life.

Hug your Special Valentine.

In the Land of OAPS

Our friend and neighbor, John, was having his eightieth birthday. His son, Johnny, was celebrating his fiftieth. They planned a dual celebration at Johnny's home in England. Of course we went. We had never been to England; another Codger and Sweet Nancy adventure! It was a three-day party! All the residents of the villagers of Northill and Ickwell were invited to partake of the delicious food, to dance to local talented musicians, and consume six kegs of select English beer. Even our neighbor, John, who at eighty, still has a good singing voice, entertained us by singing vocals from the big band era. The party included an excursion to Stonehenge and Salisbury Cathedral, which has a copy of the Magna Carta. Son, Johnny, really knew how to provide a grand time. We were worn out from the excitement.

Northill Parish is about forty-five minutes by train from London, yet it is worlds apart—much like our distance from Boston. It is small, yet vibrant, like some of our New Hampshire towns. Many people work in and close to large cities. I believe that most life happens at the edges in most small towns. In each place there are people who make things happen, so that folks in need don't fall through the cracks.

We met one such person, Leslie-Anne, family friend, and a friend to all. She was a nurse for over thirty-six years, Leslie-Anne is the inspiration for the local group of "women who run with the chickens." These women raise chickens, on a small scale of course, but those chickens are treated with tender loving care. The women meet regularly to discuss issues associated with raising chickens, like fleas, foxes, and food.

Some of these chickens are trained pets, and respond to verbal cues from their owners.

I asked Leslie-Anne, "What do you call senior citizens in England?"

She replied, "OAPs, which stands for Old Age Pensioners, of which I am proud to say I qualify." Leslie-Anne is also the chair of a caring group of villagers who provide free short-term help in family emergencies.

Leslie-Anne is married to Mike, another big contributor to village life. They have two grown children. Since Mike retired, he has driven the village transportation van, which we used to travel to Stonehenge and Salisbury Cathedral. Leslie-Anne and Mike also act in the local theater company. Mitchell is one of the village bell ringers. They are a group of villagers who meet to play the ancient nine bells in the church steeple. The tunes date back to previous centuries. Sweets was thrilled to be allowed to participate in a practice session.

People like Leslie-Anne are seldom acknowledged, elected to office, or have a street named after them. Johnny's wife, Nory, called Leslie-Anne "golden; she just shows up and gets it done." She stepped in to take John, our neighbor, to follow-up health care appointments. (He unfortunately developed a medical problem during his stay in England.) People like Leslie-Anne are seldom noticed until they are gone or have moved away.

Think of the women staffing the Council on Aging (COA) desk; think of Fred and Karen, giving until empty, then giving some more; think of volunteer COA drivers, taking folks to appointments; think Nancy and Karen, the director and the assistant. We have so many to salute and say thank you for caring. In your town and mine, we have people like Leslie-Anne who are golden in the warmth they spread. They are the heart and soul of place making our towns a community of caring. A nice place to raise children and grow old. Go visit a small town, you'll feel welcomed, even in England.

Who Is That Old Guy in the Mirror?

You may be elderly:

- When your doctor appointments become your number one priority.
- When you can't drive at night.
- When the grocery clerk carries your bags out to the car.
- When young girls open doors for you and call you "Sir."
- When the naps get longer and longer.
- When you go to still another friend's funeral.
- When you feel lucky that you can find your car in the parking lot.
- When you have to get someone to perform your normal chores, like cutting the grass and shoveling snow.
- When an attractive woman walks by and your pacemaker makes the garage door open.

On a personal note, how many of you reading this column spend just too much time like me, searching for something, and lying to our wives when asked, "Did you lose something again"

"No, Sweets, I didn't lose it, it's around here somewhere."

The pursuit of car keys, tools, papers, check books, phone numbers, grandchildren, wives, false teeth, glasses, and the list goes on and on. This does not even address names, streets, town, and words. It's on the tip of our tongue. We must have swallowed it.

Yet I can remember most of the streets in the town where I grew up, as well as my favorite teachers, best friends, ball players, and the place to get the best burgers for the least amount of money. Do you, like me, remember the smell of Sunday dinner or the taste of a favorite food like it was yesterday? Here's a pop quiz: My Mom would bake something called, snits. Has anyone else had this food?

Is the list for feeling older different for women than for men? One thing my wife mentioned was that holiday dinners are now celebrated at the daughter's or daughter's-in-law house instead of at Grandma's.

Despite popular opinion, becoming elderly is not an illness but a success story. Elderly may be a mark of a life lived so well that it has become a state of rest and reward; a time of limits in which we are forced to choose what and who are important in our remaining days.

There is sadness. We must grieve the dear friends we have lost, but there is a hint of a smile in outliving those who predicted our early demise.

The Art of Mothering

Mothering is at least 100 times harder than walking uphill backwards in a rainstorm. It's more than birthing, or as one of my female friends would say "Rabbits have babies; it takes a proud woman with courage to be a mother." It needs twenty-seven hours a day, plus a bonus eighth day. It requires patience to wait twenty years to see the results of your efforts. It's being more tired and cranky than at any time in your life. It's wearing the same clothes for years so there's enough money to outfit growing children. It's collecting cookbooks, in order to spend hours making meals for a family of food critics who have lost the path to the dishwasher. Perhaps most of all, it's finding time and space to be alone with adults who speak grown-up, as you introduce yourself by your real name, not as Susan's mom.

It is for those reasons that my first wife left town, and I became a male mother. I remember waking after five hours of twisted sheets, believing that my own mother's curse was punishing me for a being a wild child that caused premature baldness to both my parents. Gradually I learned the first names of all the nurses in the hospital emergency room. The school disciplinarian made house calls. I learned to fold laundry, help with homework, and make Hamburger Helper all at the same time.

My social life among the homegrown terrorists was reduced to begging really good-looking moms in the Laundromat for easy-cook recipes. I went to work five days a week for relief, and to bask in the warm glow of guilt. There were months I couldn't use the bathroom alone. I tried to steal an occasional solitary bath, but the neighbors complained about the crying and screaming. My kids suggested I go to my room for a time out.

Desperate, I did what any twenty-seven year-old male would do; I called my mother. It was amazing how competent and caring my mother had grown since I was eighteen. Her years of experience, two thousand phone calls, and gallons of black coffee helped us past the crisis, and she began to teach me her hard earned parenting skills. I finally had more answers than questions, and I held the family together, until I met a divorced, proud mother with her own children - a story for another time.

Turning the pages back, I remember the good times when I could hold my sleeping child and feel the love connection with each breath. I have memories of feeling the trust of my son opening a window into his world as he shared his secrets. Perhaps you too can reach back and taste the wonder of that special day when you watched your beautiful daughter, now a young woman, walk gracefully across the stage to receive her diploma, a diploma that you both worked so hard to attain. She looks across the crowd, meets your eyes; you both feel the warmth of a shared tear. Yes, you are a Mother. You've learned your art well. It's been so worth the journey!

Happy Mother's Month

I Wish I Had Known Him

Years ago when my father died, I was stunned by the number of people who crowded into the church. I never knew my father had ANY friends. How was it possible to have lived so long with a man and know so little about him? Soon after the Irish wake, I began to find the scattered pieces of the puzzle that shaped my father, and in turn the roots of my family.

This brings to mind the time a member of our weekly men's group died, who some called Mr. Computer. The men's group received a note from his wife soon after his funeral that mentioned how he loved the guys in our group. I sat next to him for years, and never heard a whisper of his affection for the men.

During the same time period, I traveled back to my childhood town to attend the funeral of a man who was one of my best friends in my growing years. One of Jack's sons told me he will forever treasure the last year of his father's life. "During his last year Dad let his hair down, and let me know him as a person." The son spoke in a hushed voice, and called that time a precious gift.

My friend, Jack, was able to do what Steve Jobs, the driving force of Apple Inc., was unable to do. When biographer, Walter Isaacson, asked Jobs, a very private man, why he wanted his biography written, Jobs replied, "I want my kids to know me." He felt he had not spent enough time with them in order for them to know who he really was.

We all know men who carry the scars of life, or of war; or who have suffered neglect or childhood abuse. In later years they have dealt with the body blows of age. Often they do so in silence. It may be a protective armor. They love deeply, but their tongues twist when they try to find words. Such men show their caring by doing, but this too often can be misunderstood. Somehow we men must find the words that are a two-way bridge to understanding. I know this affliction; just ask my grown children and Sweets.

Let me finish with a true story. Most Sundays a son visited his father, and after fifteen minutes talking of sports and the weather, they sat in silence until the mother called them to lunch.

One day the son said, "Pop, let's take a walk," So every Sunday they walked. They walked in silence, first for fifteen minutes, then an hour. One day the father said, "Fall is my favorite time of the year." Two weeks later he said, "I love English comedy," words dropped between silent walking. It went on like this for two years.

One Sunday the son did not come. A few days went by. Then the son received a phone call. It was from the man who NEVER called. "And where were you last week, not even a phone call?" The son said, "I was sick Pop, I had the flu, I couldn't even talk." From the father for the first time in his life, came these words, "I missed you. I missed our walks."

If these stories describe you, it may be time to take a walk, a car ride, or sit side by side in silence and wait for awkward words to come, one at a time. There can be intimacy in silence, but there comes a time when we need to say the words to shorten the distance between us and that man we call our father before the sands of time run out.

Summer Memories

Folks from another state who visited the beaches of my childhood were christened a special name. They were called Bennies, because they claimed they came to "The Shore" for the <u>beneficial</u> salt air and sandy beaches baked white in the sun. They seemed loud, rowdy, and dressed funny. My family was top heavy with Bennies.

Aunt Helen would rent an entire cottage at the end of a swampy road, where prices were cheap, and mosquitoes blackened the sky. The cottage was designed to sleep six; our three families would shoe horn in twenty-three. There was one bathroom! We learned to sleep through grunts, rapid fire snoring, and smells so strange your eyes wept. Identifying family ownership from mounds of blankets served as great training for raising future families. It was so much fun. It was like a yearly out-of-body experience. Cousins were so, so cool, and led such interesting lives.

Days were filled with adventure. Fathers would visit only on weekends. During the week, the mothers would lock arms in solidarity, and march us single file to the water. Each mother had a whistle with a colored cord; ours was blue, and the signal was two short tweets, one long. I blame my current hearing loss on those moments. Aunt Helen would yell "STOP, PLAY!"

So we did, bubbling red in the sun until fully toasted, then leap into the ocean waves until we turned blue. At lunch we devoured sand-filled sandwiches and bug juice. Five cents made a gallon. In the afternoon we dug deep holes, and buried bossy kids up to their necks, until discovered by a mother who tweeted for help to dig out the unsuspecting victim.

Evenings were reserved for roaming miles on the boardwalk. Bands of Bennies and locals flew like moths to the flashing lights, brassy sounds, and the excitement of the night. I had twenty-five cents, enough for an ice cream and a ride on The Plunge of Death rollercoaster. We rode it every night, and every night we were dizzy, inventing new words to describe our feelings. Life was full, and back then there were so many tomorrows. Those days, so full it was hard to breathe, we thought would live forever.

It is so much easier to feast on memories of past summers, and go hungry when life gets in the way. I find I need reminders, like my friend, a beautiful lady who learned to treasure life in a place called Lillian, but now lives in assisted living. She asks daily for someone to push her wheelchair into the morning sunshine, to catch a soft breeze to smooth her well-earned wrinkles.

She leans back, takes a deep drink of her sweet tea and sighs, "Some days are so-o-o nice; I think I'll stay around a little longer, so I don't miss anything." To this I reply, "Amen, little lady, you make everyday seem like a summer day for so many people." Borrowing a page from my friend, Joyce, summer is the time for all of us to push into the sun and savor the gentle breeze. Smile and wave to your neighbor, catch up on the winter news, and don't miss anything.

The Johnny Appleseed of Music

On one of those days that are so beautiful you forgot all aches and pains, I was wandering down the sidewalk in Fairhope, Alabama, when a turn carried me into a lush green park. I followed the sound of someone playing "Stars Fell on Alabama." Tucked into a corner, under a shade tree, on a park bench was a man bent over a guitar caressing the strings in a musical meditation. Joggers approached, stopped, jogged in place, smiled, and with a nod moved on, a little slower.

"Can I take your picture?" I asked.

"Sure, as long as I don't have to see it again," he replied.

"Are you from around here?" I asked.

"No, I'm from Rome." Then smiling at the look of shock on my face, he added, "I'm visiting my sister; Rome is in Georgia." I learned that Al Berry and his eighty dollar Morris guitar has visited 48 states, either on his Honda motorcycle, or driving his Nissan Cube.

Al Berry, at 73, speaking with the poetic cadence of a

southern gentleman, became my teacher that afternoon. He told me about Dan Emmet, a New Yorker and a member of the Bryant Minstrel Show, who was asked in 1859, to write a snappy tune to draw people into the show. He composed "Dixie," the most popular song of that era, and later a mark of pride for people of the south. Yet even in the early days of the Civil War, the tune was played by both sides of the conflict, but using different words, and solely for entertainment. The length and breadth of Al's knowledge was inspiring.

If you Google, as I did, the Eighth Regimental Civil War Band of Rome, you can read a biography of Al Berry and see a photo of him playing the drums. He has played with the unit for over 13 years. This man has had a passion for music since he was fifteen years old. He has a dream of putting some of his guitar music on the internet as a download for the over 65 crowd. Since the Sweet One and I qualified by age and listening skills, Al gifted us with a two-hour concert of the songs that touched his heart, together with the background story for most of them. He even tried to teach us about chord changes. He really tried! He also played the slow version of Dixie for us. When leaving, he gave us a copy of his CD with a promise for another set in the near future.

I recently received an e-mail. He's touring California, Washington and Oregon. Still spreading the seeds of his music. While some people get old before their time, others like Al, with purpose and passion, still hear the music and the beat heard only by them. Then there are those two states not yet seen.

Since writing this essay, Al calls me every winter when he visits his sister. Sweets, Al and I have lunch and catch up on our lives like old friends do.

The Annual Christmas Clash

I know a couple who approaches the holiday, and trims their tree, clashing like cymbals, causing friends to wonder what caused the holiday battle. He comes from a family where a smiling angel adorns the treetop, while his partner's family felt that a lighted star was correct. One believes in natural ornaments such as pinecones, dried fruit, and straw. The other treasures very old ornaments inherited from grandparents, bubble lights, and strings of shiny beads woven between the branches.

The wife wages her yearly campaign for an artificial tree instead of the traditional pine. She argues that she is tired of finding pine needles until spring. Her husband, like his grandfather and his father before him, insists on an expedition to the North Country, after the first snowfall, to find one of nature's bounties for cutting.

She wants to take decorations down the day after Christmas, so she can restore order out of chaos. He insists that the proper time is after the feast of Epiphany, a tradition honoring the memory of the three wise guys visiting the Christ child bearing expensive gifts, gifts his parents could never even have imagined owning. In the United States, it would be like the grandparents from Wisconsin coming to visit the golden grandchildren a week after Christmas, bringing gifts that parents, who are paying off their mortgage and buying sneakers, couldn't afford.

These holiday skirmishes have continued for decades, long after the children have flown the nest. I wonder if it's because we bring to our relationships the beliefs, traditions, and peculiarities we have absorbed into our souls during our growing years. Perhaps it is because we live in a society where compromise and respecting another's point of view are a sign of weakness. Sometimes it's because that's just the way we have always done things, and we tell ourselves it is too late, too much work, or too much trouble to change.

This couple, through the wisdom gained by staying together, has learned that in marriage, they have to work hard side by side, and learn to let go of old teachings in order to keep their precious union together. Besides, what would they tell their grandchildren if they decide to separate? They have learned to laugh at their differences; blend their traditions until as the days fade, they make a new tradition.

Holding his hand, she turns to him and says on the last day of December, "Well Old Man, we have survived another holiday, and we're still married."

He folds her into his arms and whispers into her ear, "Well Old Gal, my loving and patient wife, Merry Christmas. You are still my most favorite gift every year. What do you think about adding tinsel next year?"

She laughs, "I prefer angel hair." He smiles and shakes his head. So the familiar dance begins again.

May you find the gift of laughter this holiday and pass it on!

Are You Smarter Than Your Smart Phone?

I'm not a fan of change. When the deli on the corner closed, it was like a death in the family. When Sweets came home with a new hairdo, I locked the door, having been warned since childhood about strange women. I own a cell phone, but use it only if a neighbor's house is on fire.

I have been an army of one, promoting libraries with real books that you hold in your hand, and have asked others to join me in repelling the electronic invasion of our way of life. I was therefore stunned, when I walked into an early morning men's meeting carrying my 5 pound Bible, to be greeted by a circle of bald-headed guys reading from their smart phones. Is there nothing sacred?

Still reeling from that betrayal, I found the enemy hiding in my own home. The secret was revealed during a Sunday drive in the country. Sweets' purse began singing, "I am woman, hear me roar," over and over again. Sweets smiled her grandmother smile as she leaned in to shut off her phone. She informed me it was only a notice that one of our grandchildren was texting. "I had no choice since the grandchildren rejected voice communication as just so old school. Don't you want to know what's going on with OUR GRANDCHILDREN?"

Back in the day when you wanted to find a bargain, or price a car, you went down to the Last Chance Beauty Saloon or Len's Hair Clipping for Cranky Guys. Going on a trip? Call Henry down at AAA, and next day he'd send you all the maps and books you would ever need, plus add a few hints he picked up from customers. Need an answer to a question, or how to spell a word? Pull down a book, and let your fingers do the walking to the joy of discovery. If you took the time, you'd stop for coffee and conversation with a neighbor or friend, and dip into their well of experience. Both of you feeling good when you leave.

Sweets gave me an iPad one Christmas, so I am not against using computers as a tool, just not as a way of life. She did so, so I could check the weather, and read breaking news with larger letters because of my aging eyes. I wonder if she knows there is a woman inside named SIRI, who keeps asking if she can help me? Although tempted, I have yet to answer her.

There may be a few of us left, who need the warmth and excitement of the human voice, while seeking longer answers to life's mysteries. Let me remind you, we all know someone who has ALL the answers, yet when it comes to living life well, seems dumber than a bag of dead rabbits. My quest is to find those who hold close the art of conversation and the music of laughter. Those who have lived long enough to keep their laughter after overcoming great difficulty, thus earning the mantle of wisdom.

Have to go look for my cell phone; I smell smoke. Is it a wood stove, or one of my neighbors needing me?

Flight of the Codger

This past spring two of our grandchildren graduated from college. Our granddaughter was nearby in the Boston area, but a grandson out west required us to take a cross-country plane trip. But then, some would say girls are usually easier to raise than boys. Not a stroll in the park, but not an uphill marathon.

We left our warm home in pre-dawn hours to board a bus for a three and a half hour ride to Logan Airport on a parking lot, cleverly disguised as a highway. Accident, road work, or act of God? It remains a mystery. Upon arrival at the airport, we stood in a half-mile line overseen by women wearing black boots and carrying riding crops who were shouting orders in an obscure gypsy dialect. We did our best to avoid a pat down by these gals. On the bright side, we were allowed to keep our sneakers on since we were both 75 years of age. The metal detection machine did go off because of my belt buckle, but not for the box cutter I had forgotten in my front pocket.

We arrived at Gate 403b with plenty of time according to our grandchildren, three minutes! I soon heard my name paged from the boarding desk. Would my overdue library book cause a delay in departure? No, Sweets had requested a wheel chair between flights, thereby allowing early boarding with nursing infants, wounded gang members, and survivors of near fatal accidents. I had to drag a leg and mumble into my shoulder to pass the inspection of my fellow passengers.

I later asked Sweets why she had moved me from the elderly, eligible for deep discounts category, to that of feeble old guy. Using the patented wife eye-roll, she looked down on my bald head and sighed. "After the last time when you tried to run 97 gates in fifteen minutes in order to make our flight, and

I heard the death rattle in your throat. Some folks were reading magazines from your bright red face. Some people have to be protected from themselves. I am the Wife with a capital W. So give the young man a nice tip for pushing your wheel chair."

The flight never did get off on time. The mechanic had to search for a local Walmart to replace vital engine parts. However, I did enjoy being seated prior to most of the passengers. There was the man who tried to stuff his six-year old into the overhead bin to avoid an extra passenger fee; the well-dressed woman who took blankets and a headset from first class to use in economy; and the businessman who put his inflatable suitcase in the overhead bin at the front of the plane and walked to his seat in the rear. These self-centered acts were offset by the young man who changed his seat so two friends could sit together, and the young woman who put an older woman's carry-on bag in the overhead bin and loaned her a blanket she had brought from home.

If we have eyes to see, we will find those things that prove our vision of the world. I am an old man. I have seen more than my share of bad in the world, but I find, as I age, I can feel joy if I just turn my head and find a child's smile, or an old woman pulling up a blanket to cover her grandchild, to keep her safe and warm. The kiss of the warm sun on my sore back on a cold morning delights me. Then there is the hug and the light in the eyes of grandchildren who are just so glad you were there to see them on their special day when they walked proudly to the top of the stairs. Worth every mile traveled, and then some, to the proud grandparents.

An Unhurried Life

For years, every morning I would press my face against the window of the local deli, waiting for it to open; so I could scoop up my newspaper, a cup of tea, and a bagel (lightly buttered) on my way to work. Breakfast was finished when I pulled into the parking lot. Invited to parties, I would arrive early, while Frank was still in his shorts, and Maggie had yet to comb her hair. I'd set the table and go for more ice. I'd arrive so early for a departing flight, I'd have breakfast on a paper plate, drink my tea from a wax-coated cup, while reading two papers in the airport café.

On occasion my dad would look upwards and sigh, "When I retire—I'll do what I want." Dad never retired. He only stopped working when his heart gave out. My brother stopped working when he became ill. He moved by the sea to fish off the dock for sea bass. He had a few months of drinking deep from his well of happiness. The men in my family served as "good" bad examples. I was in danger of being like them; always dreaming to retire. Whatever they did, I needed to do the opposite.

They were married to the same woman all their lives; I had three wives, two of which made me healthier and better, one that taught me the words, never again. Both men had the stress of middle management, and worked in the same job; I had many jobs, from truck driver to counseling in industry. They had 2 and 4 children; I had 10. I learned to cook; my dad made scrambled eggs. Sometimes we learn lessons our families didn't intend to teach!

There have been other changes. Now, Sweets drives in order to assure that we will arrive at an airport with a comfortable cushion, so that we have enough time to pass the evil security guards. We have grandchildren who believe that time stands still for them at baggage inspection; this after Sweets sets speed records, while I sleep in the rear seat, lulled by the sound of grinding teeth.

When we are invited to a party, Sweets revs the car, while I comb the three remaining hairs on my head. I may be the only man whose women pace outside the men's restroom, waiting for me to come out. At family gatherings, the youngest child and I are the last to finish, delaying the pie parade. I have mastered the art of living in the slow lane, perhaps too well for some, but I believe it a privilege of seniority.

Some think I have slowed as part of aging, others mark the change to the moment I lost interest in politics. Perhaps they are both right, except, I think it started long ago when Sweets hid vegetables under my steak, convinced me fruits contained natural Viagra, and that regular exercise would make hair grow on my head. Then there were those bad examples. But if truth be told, I slowed down to walk the rocky road to happiness, so I would not miss the everyday moments; the colors of a sunset, a piece of music that would ease the hardest chore, the smile of a stranger. Moving quickly, we often miss what makes life worth living. Move right, into the slow lane, to see what you may have missed.

To My Sons

As I grow older, I look backwards more and more. This year, as Father's Day, or what I call National Tie Day, approaches, I remember those treasured yesterdays.

The years have reduced my short term memory to about 15 minutes, yet I remember with high-definition clarity the days on which my sons were born; or in the case of my step-sons, the day your mother allowed me to be a part of your lives. In each instance my thought was the same, "How in God's name am I going to handle this?" This was followed by a feeling of sheer terror mixed with excitement, floating into a loss of consciousness.

Over the years I have spent hours in emergency waiting rooms, and attended sports events in which I lost all sensation in my hindquarters, feet, and hands. I have refereed bare-knuckle fights between sons, listened to school concerts, trying to recognize the melody, and gave wise guidance, quickly forgotten. I have paced the floor, questioning my sanity, after I have loaned my car; picked my sons up from street corners, police stations, and friends' houses. I have driven three times the distance around the earth for family vacations, which due to selective amnesia, they claimed to have never happened.

We have fought over chores, ownership of the remote, what to eat, and what not to eat, appropriate clothes to wear visiting relatives, as well as the proper way to put lights on the Christmas tree. We have fought for the love of the same women, your mothers, never realizing they had enough to give all of us.

Your sister and I have had eruptions between us of equal intensity, but somehow through the years, we found a path to join together again. There are days when I feel close to you, my sons, while another day dawns on strangers, stranded on a distant shore, with no one knowing how to swim to the other side.

I am an old man now, and there is something I need to say to all my sons while I am still here. I know I have not always been the person you needed. I have made a barrel of mistakes. I want you to know I love you as much as I am able, and I am proud you have become responsible, caring men who have never grown so tall you can't bend down and help others. I want you to know I am grateful you have been a part of my life, and that you allowed me on your journey.

Love, Dad, alias T, alias Pop

Gaining Wisdom from
Random Acts of Stupidity

As I grow older, I am more aware of my random acts of stupidity. When I was young, I claimed a lack of experience. In my winter years I had hoped to know better, however, (sigh) let me cite but a few highlights from the last year.

One day after the men's group meeting, I put on my jacket, and on my way home stopped at the supermarket. While reaching for bananas, my right jacket pocket began to play the theme from the movie, "The Stripper." Oh no! I ran   back to the Chapin center, and discovered a guy with too much hair trying to administer a lie detector test to the exercise class. "Stop it, it tickles," I heard someone say. The class saw me, stopped and shouted, "There's your thief!" My face turned bright red. End of act 1.

Then there was the day I went to the gym, stowed my stuff, and put my lock on the adjoining locker. By the time the search party found me on the treadmill, the poor guy was already late for work. For days guys would point at me, slap their knee and chortle. If you have never been chortled at, you don't know shame. End of act 2

The final act of the year happened a few months ago. I was again in a supermarket, when I learned a family member of a man in our men's group had died. I purchased a condolence card, and at the next meeting, asked everyone to sign it. I mailed it, not to the man who suffered the loss, but to a man who resembles him. One can only imagine the surprise for the family when they opened the card. I did not realize my error until the following Monday, when this man brought a message from his relatives that rumors of his death were premature. I have been banned from sending cards of any kind.

At first I concluded people are just too sensitive. But I have since learned I must stop blaming others for my blunders, and begin to laugh more. Mistakes allow me to gain perspective, to look at my mistakes as motivation to change, and the sum of all my mistakes as Experience. All this sounds good, but I find it really hard to do.

Once a month, our men's group devotes an entire meeting to sharing experiences and mistakes, what we have done, and what we have learned. By reaching out to the other men, we help each other in this journey we call life. At our age, it's often what medicines have been helpful, treatment options, services that helped us cope with the loss of loved ones, adjustments to change in our bodies, and even on occasion, mistakes we have made and how to avoid them.

It's a new year, the slate is clean; time to get out of the house and try something new. Now why is my jacket pocket playing "Send in the clowns?"

Have a great year, may our mistakes give us wisdom and our loved ones a reason to smile.

Surviving Christmas

Unlike some men, I love Christmas shopping. Every year I clear all my plans for December 23rd, and shop until I drop. I'd go on Christmas Eve, but I don't like crowds. It gives me great pleasure to purchase gifts to make people happy. It hasn't always been that way. When my children were small, I fought with mean women who wanted the gift of the year, a gift my children were, by birth, entitled to receive. Now I start early, and for each gift I purchase for others, I buy one for myself. I therefore get what I want, every year.

I love the music of the season. With the exception of "The Little Drummer Boy," which if rumor is true, repeated playing all day will break anyone, and have him confess to crimes he cannot even pronounce. Christmas music, broadcast after Thanksgiving, gets me ready for the season. The sound of: "The 12 Days of Fast Food," "Hootenanny Holidays," or "Santa's Sleigh Sideswiping Granny" gets my spirit flowing. I do love the background harps in "Silent Wife," but Sweets has banned the hymn in our house. It took just one attempt of guy humor, and sleeping in an unheated car in a snowstorm, for me to agree to the ban.

Then there is the groaning table of food and beverage. Barbecue, covered with hot sauce on an open grill, tubs of French rries, onion rings for a vegetable, and heaps of bulky rolls for those who like sandwiches. Vegetarians bring their own food, so all are welcome. We live in the house with this year's theme written in lights on the lawn, EBENEZER LIVES! You can't miss it. Plastic cups and paper plates reduce kitchen time, where some people trade family secrets, as they do dishes. After ripping open our gifts, there's plenty of time to watch sports the rest of the day.

If, after reading the above, you laughed or said, "Oh no, he didn't!" my essay has served its purpose. I write this, because the holidays are such difficult, lonely times for many, and a brief moment of laughter is sometimes soothing to the soul. It is a season with so much to do and so little time, and it all rests on your shoulders. In the past, I have spent time alone and also in crowds, which was even lonelier. I have learned my aloneness will not change unless I change it. When we take action on the outside, we can often change how we feel on the inside.

May I suggest this year, you send a card, not an e-mail, to someone who once was important to you; that you go to a place where children are getting ready for the holidays, and allow their energy to lift your spirits. Watch Christmas shows on television, listen to music on the radio, go to community holiday events, and eat cookies not approved by your mother. Go to a church, if only to listen to the music. Don't wait until Christmas Eve when it is crowded. I once spent an entire year in a depression, unable to get past the loss of precious people in my life. I know the energy it took to just open the door and go outside. By the end of the year I learned healing needed humor and music, a valuable lesson. So turn the knob, go outside, and let the music of the holiday warm you.

Merry Christmas, thank you friends for being with us on the journey,

I Always Finish

A bank is not the place most of us go to find kindness, Southern hospitality, and stories of wonder. Then again, few banks have 86-year old receptionist, Daphne Dvorak, working full time on their staff. Ms. Daphne, besides answering the phone, comes out from behind her desk to greet you with a gentle smile, as she asks, "How may I help you today? Do you want a cup of coffee with a cookie?"

I felt like an old friend, despite the fact I only came to ask directions. Ms. Daphne introduced me to Ms. Susan, and I opened an account. Seeing Ms. Daphne as the good will ambassador of the Best Bank in Town, BB&T, is akin to passing over a diamond in the sand. Yes, the rumor is true; she has not missed a day's work in forty years, and feels fortunate to work for such a fine financial institution. But there is so much more.

In each brief visit, while taking care of my banking needs, I learned about her long distance running career. Ms. Daphne came to running late in life. "I was sixty and a half when my husband died, and I needed something to do. So for the first time in my life, I began to run." She kept running and began to enter marathons (26.2-miles).

When she wasn't running marathons, she entered 10K races (6.2 miles). She has run twenty-five marathons and five hundred 10Ks. Each time she got a printed tee shirt. She began to have quilts made from the tees. It takes forty-nine tees to make a quilt. After eleven quilts she stopped, because she ran out of storage room. Her favorite marathon was the Marine Corp Marathon held in Washington. D.C. It was her seventy-second birthday. "All those marines were lined up along the entire route, and they encouraged me to finish by singing happy birthday to me the whole time." Her eyes moistened with the wonderful memory. She cautioned me, "Of course in many races I was the only one in my age group; I could be both first and last in the same race." She chuckled, "Winning has never been my goal. I sign up, show up, do my best and finish. I ALWAYS FINISH!!"

Ms. Daphne shows up in other ways as well. No longer able to drive, she walks to the other end of town every Sunday to church, walks home, eats lunch before walking a mile to an assisted living facility to visit two elderly friends. Then she walks home again. Recently she told me she walked to a doctor in Daphne, a town eight miles away. Her doctor, concerned, asked if she needed a ride home. Ms. Daphne answered, "Why would I need that? I walked here fine, and I do know the way home, but thank you for asking."

Inspired by this 4-ft 1-inch dynamo, in a moment of madness, Sweet Nancy and I entered a 2-mile race. On the same day, Ms. Daphne entered her five hundred-one 10K. Darn, she posted a faster time! Taking a page from the Daphne notebook, we realized that as we get older, there is a new definition of winning. We take the risk of signing up and showing up. We do our best, and we Finish. As it is in the race, so it is in life. For some, this may mean visiting a sick friend, going into the hospital for an operation, finishing a chemotherapy treatment, or saying good-bye to someone. We do the right thing to the best of our ability, and we Finish, even if this means we come in last and first on the same day.

Revisit: I found Ms. Daphne still behind her desk at BB&T. She still has not missed a day in forty-five years. She has moved her residence and now walks two miles to work. She walks to church every Sunday and afterwards walks up the hill to the assisted living facility to visit the old people.

This year she fell, and was unable to participate in her thirty-second Fairhope, Alabama Spring Fever Chase. She promised to return next year, when she will be ninety-two years old. She will then be enjoying her seventy-first year in the banking business. She wanted me to know she doesn't have much money, yet she loves where she lives, and loves what she does. She invited me to come visit anytime I am in town.

Inspired by Ms. Daphne, we entered our sixth Spring Fever Chase, coming in just ahead of the police car monitor following at the end of the race. We always finish.

Till the next race, wherever that may be.

Vintage Movies

Long ago, when I was eight and a half years old, the bestest of times were steamy summer Saturdays when I entered the cool cave of the movie theatre and another world. All week I begged my neighbors for soda bottles, loaded my Radio Flyer wagon with wooden sides, pulled it across town to the Kings' super market, and collected the deposit. A valuable lesson in self-reliance. On a good week I had enough for a movie and a large bag of popcorn.

I lived in a two-movie house town; the oldest, the Brook was named after our New Jersey town, Bound Brook. It was built in 1927 as a 1250-seat vaudeville theater with an orchestra pit, five floors of dressing rooms, and a Wurlitzer organ. It was a venue as grand as our New England opera houses. It opened the same year talking motion pictures came to the silver screen. The ability to provide both forms of entertainment enabled the Brook to serve as a center for theatre for all the surrounding towns.

During the war years, a Saturday matinee cost a dime for kids. We watched two cowboy movies, such as Gene Autry, or Roy Rodgers, King of the Cowboys, with a short weekly serial like the Green Hornet, Zorro, or the scary Iron Claw sandwiched in between. Afterwards, unruly crowds of kids stumbled into the sunlight, walked into buildings, and fell off cement curbs. We felt fully alive; truth, justice, and a good horse had overcome evil. Our bellies full of popcorn, we relived the adventure until we heard the factory whistle calling us home for supper.

Wednesday was dish night. Mothers dragged their kids to the show, so that families were able to almost collect a mismatched setting for eight. Father never came, ever! You can now find these same dishes at church sales all over the country. Friday and Saturday were date nights. Teen-age boys borrowed the family car, took their special gal to the show, and remembered only fragments of the movie visible from the back row.

My older brother once went to the same movie four times, and never saw the ending. We younger kids scrunched down in front of them, making loud kissing sounds on the back of our hands, until chased by roaming ushers to the bathroom to hide. We took seriously the charge on our Captain Midnight rings to hold our nation to a higher moral standard, since we had no real understanding of the power of teen-age passion.

It is almost beyond belief that in my lifetime we can today stream movies to our smart phones or tablets anytime, anywhere, and be unaware of that time, not so long ago, when going to the movies meant traveling miles, counting nickels and pennies, and sitting down in a theater with neighbors and friends to watch. A time when containers were passed during intermission to collect money to cure polio, and Universal Newsreels informed the public about wars being fought to defend our nation. The movie house was one of the places we gathered to laugh, to cry, and to dream. A time when truth, justice, and a horse named Trigger, overcame evil and kept us safe every week, for the cost of a dime.

Life Lessons

"To leave our mark in the unset concrete of time—something to say we existed," is a line from <u>Timepiece,</u> by Richard Paul Evans, who is also the author of <u>The Christmas Box.</u>

During my short pants days, my older sister kept a daily diary protected by a ten-cent lock. One rainy day I discovered the combination, cracked it open with a paper clip, and found nothing of any value to use as a bribe. My generation writes memoirs to a generation that seldom reads anything longer than a sentence. I wonder if we have a need to leave that "mark in unset concrete," and if so, would anyone notice?

In younger years I had no doubt that I counted, but with the addition of years, I am no longer sure that I have left my mark. On a day that still sits in my memory, a small boy looked me in the eye, and in a voice that reached into my heart said, "When I grow up I hope to be like you."

I began to preen and swagger until his friend in surprise asked, "Why?"

"Because he's really, really old," answered the first boy. Another life lesson.

Perhaps some lessons are more subtle. I know a man injured in the war who swings his leg in a strange way when he walks. His daughter encourages her son to take walks with him, so he can get to know Pop-Pop. The two speak of the important things in life, the Red Sox and what flavor ice cream they will choose today. It takes but a few minutes before the young boy begins to swing his leg in a similar, strange way. When they choose their reward at the end of their walk, Pop-

Pop lets the boy order first, and says to the pony-tailed server, "I'll have the same."

There are unexpected lessons. My Granddaughter, Rena, and husband, Will, gifted me with a wee lad, Jacob by name. I have lived long enough to be a great-grandfather! I can now add the crown of great to my grandfathering title. Never having had a grandfather in my life, there is a sweet taste when I watch my son take a thousand pictures, and call me in a voice spilling over with pride, "I am so proud of Rena; she is such a good Mom. Let me tell you what Jacob did today..." When a grandfather holds his grandchild in his arms, an empty space in his heart fills. Until that moment, most of us were not aware such a vacant place existed.

There is the role of the elder as teacher. I am not sure of the duties and responsibilities of Great-Grandfathering. Perhaps I could carry on my present duties, but in a diminished capacity, since I am older. I think my primary function has been to serve as a bad example, so the parents can say, "If you make faces like that, you'll end up looking like your Grandfather, and you don't want that, for heaven's sake."

Or, "If you believe your Grandfather's stories, you will end up homeless and with a weird sense of humor." I believe my real job is to reach out a hand if life pulls one of my grandchildren down, and take the time to listen to their stories, biting my lip against giving advice. It is a sacred responsibility and a window to a world so different than my own that I am learning one shared word at a time. One of life's most treasured lessons.

Preparing for Wintah!

There is a fifth season in New Hampshire of which visitors may not be aware if they have come from "away." This season is short, intense, and necessary. We call it—preparing for wintah. (We don't pronounce the letter r).

There is a deep divide between those who call the North Country home and our treasured summah visitors. It begins with our ability to adapt to our freezing temperatures, which to us are like breathing; you notice it, but don't pay too much attention. We consider a visitor someone who has not spent 10 consecutive wintahs here, even if they have owned a house for many more years. Their stamina and loyalty are suspect; we're not ready to invite them to a sit down dinner.

This season begins when the lifeguards leave the lake beaches in September and continues until the first snow, which may be around Halloween. Do not be lulled by natives who wear shorts and a tee shirt until January; visitors have not been conditioned by long, bone-hardened cold spells, as well as the spiritual warmth from the Blessing of the Snow Blowers.

This is the time to order about five fifty-gallon drums of ice melt if you have a short driveway; you'll need more for longer ones. You need to cut and split about ten cords of wood to supplement your primary heating system. Since I am concerned about safety, I place eight-foot wooden stakes, painted orange, along my driveway, so I can find my way back home during a nor'easter. A roof-mounted searchlight is a blessing on snowy evenings. I would not follow the example of the New Jersey flatlander who planted smoke bombs to protect his mailbox from the snowplow. His road was unplowed until May, but he did buy a nifty sled, so his kids would have food and medicine. It's much more neighborly to purchase cardboard mailboxes. Ask the post office lady at the counter, she's sure to know a reliable source.

There are those among us who still remember the ice storm of 1997, also known as the 100-year ice storm. It garnered national attention, and is not to be confused with the 2008 ice storm. During the latter, as readers of this column know, I fell down a flight of stairs into the cellar, ripped the muscles from my right shoulder, and lost my job as a stunt man for AARP. During this storm, unlike the 100-year storm, the National Guard did not occupy the town; power was out for only six days, and our homegrown supermarket, Criscenti's, did not feed the 5000.

As with most natural disasters, those who were there and helped each other through the hardships, formed a special bond. It is in the reaching out that we gain strength together and know we will get through this. To this Codger, it is the source of the crusty, Yankee personality. So stick around, seriously prepare, and ask this question, "Were you here during the 100-year storm?" Prepare yourself for stories of wonder from that time when we came together, despite all our differences, remembering the true meaning of community.

I write this, days after we have been struck by another 100-year storm, Hurricane Irene. There are stories of people and towns in our area being devastated, and once again, neighbors, strangers, and folks from far away have reached out with assistance, taking days off from work and lending their skills to help to rebuild broken lives. How comforting it is to live in a part of our country where people eagerly lend a helping hand when trouble comes. I just wonder why it seems to take a major storm for us to join together.

The National Day of Eating

November is the time when we New Englanders finish our final preparations for winter. We winterize our car, start the snow blowers, and put up an extra cord of firewood, just in case. Then there is Wisconsin Sweets, who spends months filling the larder by dragging in fifty-pound sacks of flour, chasing down sales on meats and frozen vegetables to fill the freezer, which if need be, should last for the six long months of winter. You never know!

I grew up in a family where my sainted mother served blackened chicken every Sunday, and we were not Cajun. The vegetables were ALWAYS corn, lima beans, peas, and mashed potatoes, all brown. I was in my twenties before I became aware that meatloaf was not crunchy. Eggs were always scrambled, and toast tasted like charcoal. Mom was a good woman, bless her heart, but her cookbooks were missing a few pages.

I married into a family where Thanksgiving was a religious holiday. The turkey was ritually sacrificed, and offered up in prayer to our stomachs. It was a family that held up the Olympic score cards (1-10) after each course. Food was analyzed during each meal, but it was particularly intense at Thanksgiving. Loud arguments would burst upon the scene regarding the use of thyme versus rosemary. Grandma would delight in keeping it going by saying she tasted a hint of sage. We have had holiday dinners where the daughters-in-law were allowed to bring a side dish. They did so only if they consumed huge amounts of medication, or drank a quart of gin prior to the event. I was allowed to bake bread during leap year, otherwise I was entrusted to take out the garbage, to wash the pots, and to round up those football-watching lumps from the living room to assist me. Sweets was the Commander-in-Chief, cooking, shopping, making phone calls to alert the family to the upcoming holidays, birthdays, and a family member's release from prison. I served as the official greeter, taking drink orders, setting out snacks, and cleaning up.

At the time we did not realize it, but these were the golden years, our reward for raising so many strong-willed children, most of whom still speak to each other. But the seasons move on, and the page turns upon a new chapter of our lives. Sweets still loves to cook, but the celebrations are held elsewhere, in younger hands. They do the holiday well, just different. I no longer bake bread; I miss that smell of home every year. We are invited to sit at the place of honor at their table, and for that we are grateful. It was harder for Sweets than for me, but she still reigns as the queen of desserts, and the source of family wisdom.

In this time of Thanksgiving, I would like to thank all of you who read my ramblings, and who stop me in the supermarket, or while visiting the Council on Aging, and serve me kind words. Without all of you there would be no reason to write. Thank you so very much from the bottom of my wrinkled heart.

Spaghetti Love

At a meeting this past summer of the Monday morning gentlemen's gathering, I asked the men how long they had been married. The answers ranged from twenty-eight years to sixty. The total number of years came to seven hundred and eighty one! That's 781! So much for the myth that men don't commit! Of course during our twenty-eight years, Sweet Nancy thought at times I should be committed, but that's another story.

A guy's level of commitment is like making spaghetti sauce. My Maine grandson, Tim, and my wife love my spaghetti sauce. Tim calls it "wicked good." In addition to the usual spices like oregano, salt, pepper, I add my special ingredient, Garlic with a big G. How much Garlic? It's enough when you taste the sauce and your earlobes glow in the dark and are warm to the touch. Toward the end of an hour of simmering, I call the Sweet One and add a wee bit of sugar. Nancy is a master cook, and besides being my Sweet One, gives a thumbs up or down before suggesting improvements. Then, like our marriages, it must sit for a long period of time so that the ingredients can blend together.

Years ago, we Monday morning men of the Chapin Center found our special ladies, built couple lives, then family lives, and now in the autumn of our lives have well seasoned relationships, and we are still cooking. It fills us up like no other in our lives.

I want to take this space to give a heartfelt round of applause to our special ladies, our wives, who have been the secret ingredient in our lives. Your man may never have learned the language from his father to say the words, but we hear the stories of your blessings. Thank you all from the bottom of our wrinkled hearts.

THOMAS DONNELLY

Momma Weather:
Only the Best for You

There are some people for whom the weather forecast is both an event and a passion. Sweets loves to surf the world of weather, starting with television's dawn forecast, and ending with its evening predictions. In between, she checks her smart phone. She keeps a daily journal of high and low temperatures, times of sunrise and sunset, wind speed, barometer, and humidity. Last she determines the strength of the sun on her personal Sweets Sunshine Index. Given a few minutes to consult her material, she can tell you all you need to know about a specific day for the past decade. She is married to a man who will wake up, walk out the door while he is wetting his finger, proclaiming when he returns, "Sure is cold out there, yes sir." Or, pulling on my left ear, I predict, "Feels like rain."

Yet if I ask her what the weatherman said about tomorrow's forecast, she can't remember. I blame it on the local weathermen's voices. The only time these guys show any excitement is when it has rained forty days and forty nights, or when a nor'easter with the name, "Vengeance of Thor," is headed in our direction. At the other extreme are the chirpy chicks wearing outfits designed by Ladies of the Evening R Us. We don't remember their forecasts either. We need someone to command our attention. We need someone like our Momma.

Enter Bernice, a round woman with a wide smile, wearing an easy wash, classic pants suit with a white blouse. Her graying hair has a blue tint. She delivers the weather from WMOM. Bea earned her degree in meteorology while raising five children. She might start the forecast like this: "Good morning, Honey, did you get a good night's sleep? Why don't you fix yourself a cup of coffee before you start your busy day? Come in and sit with me. I will tell you the forecast, so you can plan your day, cause you're so special, despite the rumors I heard at the coffee shop. Those people are just so jealous.

"It is gonna be a pretty day in Momma's neighborhood. We are going to start with a little fog, but hey, that's a good thing. Fog will provide moisture for the plants you put in last weekend. Are you and the children eating a good healthy breakfast? Don't give me that nonsense you don't have time to feed your precious children. A healthy breakfast will keep you away from those coffee break doughnuts. Bless your heart, you try so hard to lose those fat pounds without a lick of success. I only remind you cause I love you so much. Anyway, it's chilly, about 45 degrees, but the fog should burn off by ten o'clock. The temperature should rise to the normal high of 70 by three o'clock. So dress in layers, and bring your umbrella; there is a 20% chance of rain. This may not sound like much to you young folks, but I say it's better to be safe than sorry.

Just remember, it's time to buy your mother or your wife a Mother's Day card. If you forget again, there will be plenty of thunder and storms for weeks to come. So long, until six o'clock; when I will have more caring weather for you and the family. I hope you have a beautiful day. You deserve it! Remember Momma Weather, always current, because we love you and want you to be safe. If you can't trust your Momma, whom can you trust?"

Brought to you by

Codger Tom, and Sweet Nancy, censor and editor

THOMAS DONNELLY

My Wife Married an Alien

My wife, Sweets, and I have been incompatible for over 30 years. She thinks like a woman, acts like a lady, and hits like a German kick-boxer. I do not have any of those traits. Think manly man, with all the baffling traits that entails. There is also the religious issue. She is a Hindu Presbyterian, and I am a Buddhist Baptist. She loves vegetables, whole grains, and any drink that ends with the word juice. My people believe that ice cream, chocolate, and Guinness constitute three of the five major food groups. Sweets is able to remember the names and birth weight of third cousins. I need a wall chart with the names and ages of my own children. She is an early morning person, hitting the floor and singing, ready to start the day; I come fully alive when the sun goes home, and I hear the smoky sound of late night radio.

We came together because of the children. We were each raising a cell of terrorists. People would close their car windows, or take another way home, rather than drive by our house. To some in the outside world, they looked like ordinary kids, but we knew better. We were trapped in the parental sentence, without the possibility of parole, or a locked bathroom door. We needed relief, rest, and the possibility of a long-acting tranquilizer. We married instead.

We were months into the marriage before we discovered we had married an alien. Then it got worse; the families took sides; nine children on one side, and two wobbly parents on the other. We stayed together, because we had a dream, or was it something we ate? I don't know. In any event, we won. They grew up and moved out. We moved and enrolled in the witness

136

protection program, so they could not find us until they had grandchildren.

If our grandchildren would listen, I would tell them that long-term relationships, like marriage, are a series of gains and losses. You don't get everything you want, but you get what you need, even if at first you bite a hole in your lip. You drive stations wagons or vans instead of sports cars. You give up the speedboat, but in return, have someone who catches your arm when you stumble, or believes in you, even after your mother has given up hope. You have a partner who comes out in the middle of the night when you have had an accident, drives you home, and tells you, "We'll get through this." Perhaps the hardest task is adjusting when your partner thinks, speaks, and behaves differently than you do. They are not trying to get you upset; they just are not you.

I would tell my grandchildren that they live in a different world, where women often get advanced degrees and much of the stress of the work world. Grandson, you may have to learn new ways to be a stand-up guy, different from anything your dad ever thought about. For years one could see the heel marks of guys of my generation, who were forced to attend our daughters' dance recitals. Now dads put their photos in their gym lockers.

Learn to love your alien, they know all your secrets, and have never told the grandkids.

Climbing the Digital Mountain

I have always admired and have been willing to learn from older women. I have attempted to learn from older men, but they tend to refuse eye contact and growl, "read the damn manual, or go watch a YouTube video." My comfort with older women began with Miss Schick, my second grade teacher, who rewarded us by reading a story. I knew she was reading the story just for me, because she looked at me, smiled and called me a special name, "Hey You, Chubby, stop wiggling and bumping your head on the desk!" The other kids were just wallpaper! Unfortunately, Miss Schick had to leave before the end of the year, because she swallowed a watermelon, or so I had been told.

For most of my life I have been a high maintenance learner, and older woman seem to have more patience or, perhaps, lower expectations. I come from a line of men skilled in turning wheels and knobs, pressing buttons, adjusting dials, using screwdrivers and hammers. We love a clear, well-written manual. These skills do not transfer in this digital age, where we go for help by touching a screen, or waiting on the telephone an hour, in order to speak with someone who uses English as his third language, and pronounces his name Wack, like in Jack.

Grandchildren are wonderful, but love us so much, they do it for us. They can't teach us, since they have been digital since birth. Enter an older woman, Computer Annie, who comes into my winter class of hairless men and ladies with hearing aids, pushing a walker. She has vision problems, which require large print manuals and an overhead projector. She hands out printed instructions for her class, "Riding Your

138

iPad." Her patience with my people makes Mother Theresa look like a slacker. She knows that her students love the smell of books, dance the slow tunes, and that repeating instructions is a form of teaching. Some take her class again and again. She makes us believe climbing the digital mountain is no harder than raising children, or making a marriage work for fifty years. She shows us the benefits; we can make the letters larger so we can read books easier, download videos of the family, send free e-mail across the miles, and use something called an app to find out the weather forecast, the latest news, and more.

I'd like to finish with a story. A 90-year-old woman came into a store once a week for supplies, always upbeat despite the weather outside. Curious, one stormy day the owner asked her how she had lived so long with such a positive outlook, despite the troubles she had obviously seen during her long life. The woman smiled, then said, "Everyday I spend my time finishing one or more projects, and every morning I start a new project. So far it's working."

Some of us live fully, others just count the days. It's been a long winter. Time to call a friend for lunch, plan your garden, or begin a project you have been putting off.

Family Reunions

In my family we did not have reunions, we had wars. We traveled long distances to the site of battle. Confined in heavy steel traps before air conditioning, we had warm-up skirmishes in the back seat of the car. "Ma, he hit me." "Ma, she's touching me, and won't stop." After hours of whining, Ma would uncoil her arm, flick her wrist, and catch the whiner on the ear with a sharp fingernail. In other families, you would receive a tongue-lashing; in ours, only a physical injury caught our attention. Sniveling lasted only about three minutes before someone broke the cease-fire. This continued the entire trip, until we arrived with swollen eyes from lack of sleep, unwashed faces streaked with sweat, ready to meet our opponents: *The Relatives*.

The clans gathered so infrequently that most of us did not recognize members of other families. Our distrust was based only on rumors and family lore spread by the aunties who had been burning up phone lines for years in order to fan the flames. The list of offenses was long: forgetting birthdays, bawdy Christmas letters, adult children sassing their parents, marrying outside the faith, adultery, and public drunkenness. Most of the black marks happened before we had been born. The fall-out was always the same; warnings on how we were to behave, and the deafening sound of silence until the oldest generation died or moved to Canada.

Not everyone heeded the warnings. There was my young cousin, Kate, who despite frequent warnings went to visit Grandma on a Friday, the day after payday, without calling first. Before 10am! She came home early, drank two quick shots of whiskey, and smoked a pack of unfiltered cigarettes.

She had never smoked or drunk before. But then she was only twelve years old at the time.

A year after Sweets and I were married, she brightly announced that we were going to Wisconsin, to the 5-year family reunion. I felt my life go down the drain, while the room spun like a carousel. NOOOOO! Don't do this to us! It will kill our marriage, give the kids PTSD, and cause the dog to be possessed by Lady Gaga. Sweets, a mother of four wild children, pulled the ultimate wife weapon, "Don't you love me? Don't you love the children?"

I know men who took back a deposit on a boat for which they had been saving since they were seven. Instead they used it to remodel the kitchen, because they did not answer that question quickly enough. I tried to weasel out, but one hot summer day, I found myself driving our air-conditioned station wagon to Wisconsin, wild children caged in the back.

To my surprise, it was a family gathering, filled with laughter, food and drink, instead of fighting. It is hard to fight when your mouth is full, dancing the polka, or people round you are sleeping, due to Milwaukee's best brews. I learned bratwurst is made in 15 different flavors, and if you hope to have a full life, you have to let go of the past. We went to six more reunions, and stopped only when the older generation died or moved to Canada. I can, these years later, still taste those Midwestern memories, and hear the change in Sweets voice when she calls family across the many miles, going home again.

The Night I Stole the Christmas Tree

When my family sits around the kitchen table on cold December days, reaching back in our cluttered memories to Christmas past, we often speak of the lean times, when our money was shorter than winter daylight.

We remembered those times when we spent an entire day, or so it seemed, breaking paths in frozen snow looking for a Christmas tree. Legs as heavy as lead, our frozen fingers cupped inside mittens, we would shout in the frosty air, "This is the perfect tree, let's go home." Mother would whisper, "Just a little more, just a few more trees to consider." We boys and men would shake our heads and trudge up the hill, just a little more, just to make her smile. Each and every time we pointed to another perfect tree, it was rejected, a cold lesson in patience and endurance.

There was the year a winter storm knocked out electric power on our street, and only on our street. A family across town made room in their second stove for our turkey. To this day we all remember the Christmas when we missed the smell of roasting turkey, flavored with evergreen.

We groan when we recall the Christmas Eve the cat attacked the tree top angel, and all of grandma's ornaments from the old country met a premature death. There was a certain sound from that event that some of us still hear. It brings back the people who shared an old-time holiday, and of a grandma who claimed her people were the first to bring the Christmas tree to America.

Finally, there was the Christmas secret I kept buried for fifty years. It all started, if memory can be trusted, during one of those lean years when there was more month than the sum of my paycheck. We were a family of five, living in the country, five miles from any town. I planned to wait until Christmas Eve to purchase a bargain tree on my way home from work. What I didn't plan on was the blizzard that visited on my trip home. Somehow I found Cheap Al's tree stand in the middle of town, but no Cheap Al. In desperation I took a tree, intending to return the day after Christmas and pay him.

There were no other options; the storm had become a whiteout, and it was getting dark. As punishment, my car slid into a ditch, and I had to drag that darn tree the last half mile home. When I returned two days later, the tree stand was an empty lot piled high with leftover trees. I wonder if the statute of limitations has run out, or will my deed haunt me like Scrooge? In my defense, the crime has never been repeated.

This year, as in other years, our family stories will not be about gifts we received, but about unique behaviors that made us different from other families, and the love we shared. On some days there is a certain smell, a sound of church bells in the distance, and a special way the light catches in the grandchildren's eyes—and it all comes back.

Merry Christmas and Happy New Year.

Guys and the Love Month

February 14th is a day set aside to honor Saint Valentine, a martyr who lived in the 3rd century CE. As the story goes, the Roman emperor, Claudius II, set forth a decree banning marriage for young men, as he believed it weakened them, and made them poor soldiers. Valentine, a priest, was unable to marry, but in public argued with the emperor about his decree. Although he presented a brilliant argument, he lost the case and his life. Smart men have been losing such skirmishes for years, particularly when it comes to Valentine's Day. I offer you a few examples, drawn from the lives of friends.

Example 1: The husband, a true romantic, knowing his wife's love for chocolates, gave her two pounds of Swiss dark chocolate.

Wife: "Are you trying to make me fat?"

Husband: "No love." (On the inside he thinks) *Why would I want to do that? If you gain one pound we eat tofu and carrots for two weeks.*

Example 2: Wife: "Don't buy me anything for Valentine's Day this year. We can't afford it." Husband heeds her words and doesn't buy her anything.

Wife: "Not even a card!!! How about a single flower? I'm sure if you gave up one game of golf, or one lunch with your buddies, you might buy something—something—anything. What will I tell my friends and your mother?"

Husband: (on the inside he thinks) *You claim I never listen and yet when I do—I think I'll go into the garage, and hit myself in the head with a hammer.*

The above may not be your stories. The Sweet One just expects me to remember and give it my best shot. A single flower in hard times, more adventuresome gifts at other times. Last year I gave her a shovel, so she could dig her own garden.

So Guys, don't give up. She won't gain weight on flowers, and if you take her to a low budget cafe, she can have a salad, and you can have something with lots of raw meat. Take her hand, look her dead in the eye, and smile; it will make you look interesting, or at least like you're paying attention. Remember St. Valentine. Despite his skill in presenting his case, he lost the argument and his life. Dare to break this self-destructive tradition of trying to win, when we don't even know the rules. Try to remember why you chose your lady those many years ago, and smile. Was it love or lust? I can't remember, but I want the journey to continue in peace and harmony. Even if you think you win, you sleep alone.

Now & Then

When I was eleven and knew everything worth knowing, my family lived in New Jersey, in a town a mile square, that was so cramped there wasn't room for snow. Trucks were loaded, driven to the river on the edge of town, and the snow dumped, like so much garbage. The main street merchants, already short of parking spaces, viewed snow as a drain on the economy.

On the other hand, my friend Jack and I saw those icy flakes as white gold. We not only had the day off from school, but we could spend the entire day shoveling sidewalks for widows and tired old men. There were even days when we could earn ten dollars apiece, plus a bonus of hot chocolate and a side dish of cookies. When you are young, snow is always good! Every time it snowed in my town, I could hear music in my head, cha-ching, cha-ching.

Now, I am one of those tired old men from long ago. The snow has become heavier. I have developed a dependence on my friend, my snow blower, Big Red. Red is able to throw snow twenty feet or more, much further than a small boy. I wonder if snow blowers increase testosterone for men, since the guys in my neighborhood while working, will clench their right fist, and raise our arm in the air in greeting; the Olympic salute! Hoo-Raaaa! Hoo-Raaa!

In that town of long ago, before the radio was finished forecasting snow, there would be a steady stream of people walking to the grocery store, stripping the shelves of milk and bread. A few candles, a glass milk bottle filled with water, a loaf of bread and we were ready! That was winter in New Jersey! In my New England town the app beeps on the iPhone,

SUV's form a conga line into town to purchase wine, cheese and crackers. On the return trip, they stop for gas for the generator, call a few friends, start a bonfire in our neighbors fire pit, and hold a winter carnival. That's winter in New Hampshire.

This is a humor column, I am well aware that our winters are long and sometimes arduous. Yet my friends, I have personally experienced how we as a community can come together, reach out to those struggling, and make that load a little lighter. I write to bring up a warm memory or a smile to those who look forward to longer days and sunshine. This winter will soon fold into our memory book. For each season there are lessons to be learned, new stories to be shared, and new friends not yet met. Have you noticed most of the interesting stories we tell our grandchildren have been when we have overcome some difficult period in our lives? Some are even true.

My Wife Left Me

Occasionally Sweet Nancy will leave me alone for days without direct supervision. The operative word is direct. A message in wife-speak is passed among the female relatives. Within a day of Sweets' departure to visit grandchildren or her Wisconsin siblings in order to take command of another kitchen, the phone calls begin. Our daughter wants to know if I am eating enough vegetables, and if I have enough fiber in my diet. A daughter-in-law wants to know if I am getting enough sleep and exercise. Then Sweets' ninety-two year old aunt in Kansas City calls to find out if I am lonely or depressed.

Despite my carefully concealed lies, the accurate answer to all these questions is NO! I am eating food on the wife's forbidden list, playing loud country crying songs, watching racy movies until late into the night, and my only exercise involves walking to the mailbox for the latest Netflix video. In short, without supervision I have regressed and am living like our bachelor son. At seventy-eight, how cool is that!

At other times I wander through life with a sign on my back visible only to certain women. A strange woman walks up to me while I am tying a loose shoelace and gives me instructions. Others give me advice on posture, wardrobe, and table manners. One woman in a southern state stopped traffic on a busy street so I could walk across. She smiled sweetly, and said, "Maybe someday when Ah get really old, someone will do this for me." My wife watched the entire situation as she dodged oncoming cars. I know this does not happen to other men, since I never heard anyone talk about it.

One friend said, "You are a real chick magnet! Here you are bent, old, and wrinkled, and all these women give you their attention. I am so jealous." Then he looked at me funny and said, "Here, let me button your shirt, you missed one."

Whatever I've got, now guys have noticed it.

The Final Party

I wonder if there are others like me, who as we grow older and lose friends, think about the end of life. I exercise, eat a healthy diet, take my meds, follow doctor's orders, and think pure thoughts. Well, the last one is a work in progress. While I am delaying the end as long as possible, the last dance does creep into my thinking.

So I am planning the final sendoff, and making it a matter of public record, so that Sweet Nancy cannot change the agenda. In addition, I want to support her in her efforts to rebuff our strong-willed children. It is my party, after all!

I do want a church service where the minister starts off with a few knock-knock jokes; tells the modern version of the Prodigal Son; and lies wildly about my contributions to society and mankind. The choir sings a few gospel hymns with the audience, as they clap hands marching out of church.

I want a cherry wood coffin (sanded smooth as a baby bottom) set up at the entrance to the room for the departure dinner. I want to be dressed in a red shirt, with one of my bolo ties. I want to wear one of those red sponge clown noses, so that people who file by will laugh and remember all those times we have enjoyed together.

At the departure dinner, while feasting on pizza, sausage with onions and peppers, meatloaf, fried chicken, and the nectar of my homeland, kegs of Guinness, I want everybody entertained by my extended family at the Sunapee Coffee House. Sweets will add the vegetables as she sees fit. On that day there will be no calories, as long as you eat standing up.

It is my hope that those gathered can swap remember when stories and say, "You know, he wasn't really too bad." I hope that my wife and family know how much they have contributed to the joy in my life. I am so grateful for their love, as well as their ability to accept one or two minor faults buried in me. They will be glad to reveal them, now that I can't retaliate. Just remember, St. Peter and I are buddies, and he has the keys to heaven!

Wooden Desk Days

I started school in a small town in New Jersey. It was a parochial school run by a black robed Swat team, the Sisters of No Mercy. Thumping, as a tool of learning, was encouraged. If we made the mistake of ratting on the black robes, complaining they hit us for "no reason," our parents gave us a reason and hit us again. There are people you pass on the street who keep their hands in their pockets to hide scars on their knuckles made by 12-inch rulers with metal edges. We were taught we could take our troubles to God, or was it the president? I forget. Anyway, neither answered my phone calls.

This was a school system with little money. Parents paid tuition or applied to their local church for help. Since I was an unruly child, my parents paid the ransom—willingly. We had dimly lit classrooms and textbooks held together with adhesive tape. Eighth-grade boys wearing white straps acted as crossing guards. They loved the power of stopping adults in their cars, making them wait until given the signal.

We were a community of fund-raisers. Hordes of students were hurled at the townspeople on a regular basis. We sold expired garden seeds in ugly green packs, obscure magazines that listed religious retreat centers, and statues that glowed in the dark. We were pitted against each other in order to become the most blessed number one seller.

This was a different time. Sweets went to a Lutheran school that also believed sparing the rod spoiled the child. I have friends who went to private and public schools that believed corporal punishment was a soldier in a child's army. There were some kindnesses. One black robe taught me to throw a curve ball. Another stroked my hand when my dog died. From them I learned small acts of kindness can last a lifetime.

The following is

A PUBLIC SERVICE ANNOUNCEMENT

From

Codger & Sweets

THOMAS DONNELLY

A PUBLIC SERVICE ANNOUNCEMENT

Do you, or someone you know, shout, shake your fist, and make death threats during sporting events on television? Do you own one or more golf clubs twisted beyond repair from frustration on the golf course? Do your wife and children lock themselves in a soundproof room during the nightly news. Does your one remaining friend call you cranky? You may be the victim of IMS also known as Irritable Male Syndrome. (check Wikipedia)

IMS, also known as Dels Syndrome, was discovered some years ago by Dr. Lincoln in Edinburgh, Scotland. Makes one wonder if wearing kilts in winter made Scottish males more testy than men in long pants. The primary reason for the affliction is a reduction in testosterone levels, which occurs in all males after the age of thirty. A few symptoms are anger, social withdrawal, lack of identity (retirement?), depression, mood swings, and some guys have hot flashes! Male Menopause, The Musical?

The syndrome can be brought on by poor diet, (single men), excessive alcohol consumption, (your brother-in-law) having an operation, lack of sleep (guys who fall asleep during a ballet), and LACK OF SEX. I knew it! Not enough sex can make you sick. We guys having been complaining for years, now we have evidence. Why do I hear women chortling and slapping their knees as I write this? I hope they have more sympathy for the guy who has hot flashes.

While some would see IMS as a debilitating affliction, causing men to sit in their recliners, doomed to growl at the television, and complain about the younger generation, (which at our age is a substantial part of the population), I suggest it is an opportunity to connive. Conniving is an old guy skill we learned from our children as we watched them deal with their mother. For example:

Ever Loving Wife:

"Jim and Doris Terrible have invited us for dinner; behave yourself this time and don't talk politics."

Cranky:

"You'll have to go alone, I'm having a wicked IMS attack."

Cranky:

"Let's go make whoopee."

ELW:

"My head hurts and my back aches; not tonight fella."

Cranky:

"Maybe you could take a Jumbo Strength Pain Pill, so I don't get sick. Remember the last time I had an IMS episode, the neighbors put up an eight foot fence, which I enjoy, but the shade killed your roses."

I am sure that if we turn off the TV, give up golf for 90 days, (January through March) and give a large donation to the Council on Aging if they will all root for the Sox this year, we can overcome this latest threat to our usual gentlemanly dispositions.

That's Not Funny, Honey

As I began work on this column, I asked my wife, "If I'm an old codger, can I call you a codgerette?"

"Only if you have a death wish," she replied. What I thought was a connection, she regarded as an insult. This kind of talk can develop into a source of major misunderstandings between men and women.

We males consider the insult an art form to be honed and appreciated. We readily describe our older best friend as so old he was ten years old when the Dead Sea Scrolls were just getting sick. We describe another friend as so lazy he thinks that manual labor was a Spanish man. We have been known to ask a terminally ill friend, "If you die, can I have your golf clubs?"

If this is how we connect with friends, how do we treat others? We just don't pay close attention to them.

Trouble looms like a New England ice storm when we apply the same standards to women and children. For example, the guy who sent his pregnant wife diet pills at the baby shower. Then there was the father who tied dead minnows to his son's kite for balance at the Fourth of July family picnic. The man was stunned that anyone was angry! He thought it was hilarious.

Guys, rather than inhibit our quirky male humor, we need to meet with other men who are not offended, and can appreciate the unique flavor of the male funny bone. We need a safe place where we are understood and applauded for our zany, fun-filled unique sense of humor. A place where you never hear, "That's not funny, honey."

Ladies, send your guy to a men's group, golf foursome, the gym, or anyplace where he can get his humor out with other quirky guys. If we have our type of fun, we'll be so much fun to be with for you and yours.

Keep smiling and tell everyone how much you love the cold. It will make your family wince and men smile. The saying "Whatever doesn't kill you makes you strong," must have come from a guy smiling through pain.

The Summer Jubilee

"Jubilee!" A call mixed with the cry of the seagulls in the half-light just before dawn. "Jubilee! Bring your buckets; it's here!" Jubilee is an unpredictable, natural phenomenon that takes place in the shallow shoreline of Alabama's Mobile Bay along a fifteen-mile stretch between Point Clear and Daphne. It's a celebration and a feast of the sea for local residents, who harvest hundreds of flounders, blue crabs, and shrimp, filling buckets and washtubs. It occurs here and nowhere else in the U.S. It is caused by "a lack of oxygen in the bottom water, forcing bottom-fish and crustaceans ashore." (Auburn University study) It is a time to call family and friends together, a time to feast on nature's bounty.

Jubilee. It can be defined as a stroke of good fortune, revelry, or a celebration. We may not live on that small strip of land in the south, but we can celebrate the summer gifts of our lives. It was a long cold winter; spring in my yard was filled with frequent, chilly rains. Summer is here. Children and grandchildren have graduated. We have traded wool and polartec for shorts, tank tops, and bathing suits. The heaviness of winter is locked in the closet.

And the harvest is in—time for our Jubilee, our celebration. Unpredictable, at the whim of weather conditions, it must be harvested quickly. Sounds a lot like gardening. Some years the deer, rabbits, and raccoons invite themselves to dine after you did all the hard work, and leave you with slim pickings and the chore of cleaning up. Then there are the jubilee years; if you don't lock your car doors, the garden elf fills up the front seat of your car with zucchinis, or tomatoes, or lettuce. It's all good!

In my corner of the world, it is a time when men don aprons and throw huge pieces of raw meat on the grill. Backyards resemble the smoking chimney of steel factories, when we were self-reliant and a world leader in manufacturing. The old days that we mature (old) guys talk about. Summer is when we gather the clan together, tell lies, and eat gallons of ice cream. We sit around campfires and go fishing.

We make friends with our new neighbors and invite them over for a cookout. It is the vacation we take, a reward for all the months we worked. It is the time when the summer visitors return, making yearly contributions to the local economy, and for that we are truly grateful. We thank God for sunshine, so we can take long walks, and hike in our beautiful forests. We can cut grass without a shirt, and enjoy the soft breeze. *Note: This gift does not apply to granddaughters.

May I never grow too old to enjoy warm tomatoes from the farmers market and the taste of sweet corn smothered in butter. May I treasure each day above the grass as a gift. It's Jubilee time; enjoy the summer bounty.

Grandma Power

There was a time and place in my growing years that now sit on a special shelf in memory. Even now, these many years later, when the light is right, and there is a smell of garlic and tomato sauce, I remember Grandma. She wasn't my real Grandmother. On Drake Street, our one-block neighborhood, she was simply known as Grandma. This Grandma was the round, neighbor lady who picked me up between her garlic smelling breasts, and her laughter burst like thunder, as she held me to her apron and stroked my back with floured hands. I held on for the ride. Grandma adopted me and called me Boy. As the years passed, she called me Tommy Boy.

In my world across the alley, we lived in a second floor apartment above the landlord, and I was required to be quiet. I tried, I really tried to walk softly on hardwood floors, not to wham the screen door, or drop my shoes with a thud. At most, I lasted an hour, and then Ma would sigh, "Tommy, you've got to play outside." She didn't want trouble, and knew I needed to run off all my boy energy.

Outside, I sniffed and smelled spaghetti sauce, and my nose led me to Grandma's door, like a moth to light. I knocked and heard her voice boom from the other side, "Come in Boy, what, ya knock? You gotta come right in. My house yorra house."

Grandma sat at the table drinking black coffee with ladies from the neighborhood who were humming with the latest scandal. Grandma just nodded, looked up, and smiled at me. It seemed that Grandma was always at her command post, twirling a huge wooden spoon between two giant, boiling pots. She moved like a symphony conductor, dipping one hand into

160

containers of oregano, basil, and pepper, while the spoon, like a baton, beat a rhythm against the sides of the pots, one filled with water, the other dark red sauce. At times she stopped, dipped her spoon, tasted, sighed, smiled, or groaned in Italian and frowned, then began the music again.

I stood there watching the steam cling to the ceiling, while hearing the gurgle in the pots, and in the background, the hum of ladies in flowered housedresses and black ankle-high shoes. Grandma pulled the stool from behind the stove, sat down and said, "Boy, sit! How's your momma?" Then she waited for the required report on her and the rest of the family. Soon she pulled me onto her wide apron, stoked my hair, and asked, "And how is Boy today?"

She had only a few remaining teeth, her gray hair danced wildly on her head, and her face had deep holes. But when she heaped my plate with the smell of Italy disguised as red sauce on pasta, looked down, and smiled, she was so beautiful. I am not Italian, but Irish; but for five short years I was Italian, and for the first and last time, I knew the smell and touch of a grandma, as well as special grandma love.

In Search of the Perfect Gift

My wife, Sweets, recently had a birthday that she vowed not to celebrate. I gave myself the task of buying her something that would bring a smile to her face. I must have spent ten minutes, maybe more, looking through the catalogs for the perfect gift. Last year, the chain saw I purchased to help her saw firewood did not make her happy. Out of the blue, I had my once-a-year brilliant thought. Sweets loves to garden, so why not a garden ornament that would set off all her hard work? I placed my order three days prior to her birthday, giving the reliable US Mail plenty of time to deliver. The gift arrived exactly on her birthday, perfect!

I was so excited, anticipating the look of joy on her face that I almost dropped the large machete I handed her to open the box. Upon opening, Sweets had the look she reserves for bloody car crashes we see on the highway. "My God, what is it? Should I call the bomb squad?" she shouted. I looked. Oh, no! The Delight Your Wife Gift Company had reached into the ugly bin, and sent three glow in the dark globes designed to frighten crows and small children. Although the company sent a replacement within days, I have noticed Sweets locks the bedroom door and sleeps with a night light next to the bed. It is no wonder that Delight Your Wife told us to keep the first gift and never send it back.

I still wonder if this incident was a factor in her dark mood a few days later. She informed me she was slowing down. She said this after she returned from walking a mile to and from the gym for her one-hour high impact yoga class. "Codger, before my birthday I would take two classes, and then lift weights. She sighed and would have said more, but she had to make four-dozen doughnuts for a fundraiser for the Kick Your Butts Ladies Guild. They were raising funds for children too poor to own a smartphone. I would have offered words of encouragement, but I was busy pouting over the fact that I don't have a smartphone, so I just took a nap before we split firewood for the afternoon. Getting old just wears you out.

Please keep in mind this is a humor column, the truth is in there somewhere, hidden among some slight exaggerations. What is true from my viewpoint, is that when someone we love is going through difficulties, we want to take away the pain. Sometimes by buying something that we think will make them happy again. This seldom works.

We all have transitions, which are painful and confusing. Our children grow up, leave us to start lives of their own without us. They make mistakes, and have to work it out without our help, in order to grow. We grow older, changing mentally and physically, forcing us to adjust. We survive, and some of us find new ways to thrive. I know from all the years we have spent together that Sweets is a Thriver. Sometimes the most perfect gift we can give is to be a cheerleader to our loved ones on their solitary journeys.

Spend Thanksgiving with someone that makes you smile.

International Grandchildren

One warm Sunday evening this past summer, Sweets and I traveled to Newport, NH, where on the stage, a band of gray beards, called the Flames, reached back in time to play "Mr. Tambourine Man," by Bob Dylan. Across the curve of the green lawn, white heads, folded into lawn chairs, swayed and smiled, mouthing the words they learned long ago, so that the lyrics come as easily as breathing.

When the band changed direction, swinging into "Light my Fire," by the Doors, it lit a flame in a small group of college-age kids, who had been selling slices of pie as a fundraiser. They jumped up and started to dance in front of the bandstand. This prompted some gray heads to leave their popcorn-selling booth to join them; the music became a path joining the generations.

These students were on a mission from Volunteers for Peace. Their leader was Charon Urban, a social studies teacher from Newport High School, who has devoted considerable effort for the last twenty-eight years to lead such camps. The students were from Azerbaijan, China, France, Germany, Italy, Russia, South Korea, and Spain. Their mission: to repair pre-arranged projects, to foster an understanding of their countries, and to share back home what they learned from the average citizens of our country.

A few days later I met the students and Mrs. Urban at lunch with the seniors at Newport Nutrition Center. One or two students sat at each table. I watched as a blonde German girl stroked the hand of one woman, while speaking German to her, thus feeding the older woman's hunger to hear the language of her childhood. A gentleman, Arthur, was seated between two smiling Korean girls who were exchanging views on education.

At my table a charming student, Zulfiyya from Azerbaijan, held our attention by speaking about food. We were surprised to learn that her country, so close to Turkey, preferred tea to coffee. She told of her studies at her university, located in Germany. It seems that travel between countries is as frequent as our travel between states. She winked, and said she even had an Irish boyfriend who loved to eat, which was lucky for both, since she was a number one cook. This caused much laughter.

At the end of the meal, Wan Fang, from China, played a classical piece on the old piano; sometime later, another student from Germany played jazz on the same piano. Bastia, from Russia, found a bottle and a wand, and blew bubbles while we tried to catch them. The room filled with laughter in every corner.

There are endless meetings held each year, countless dollars spent, expensive experts consulted, and thousands of miles flown in order to promote communication with people from other nations. I wonder why we could not learn to cross the bridge over the canyon between us by using the power of grandparent love and understanding. I was privileged to watch that bridge being crossed that day, over and over again, despite the differences in language and culture.

In the sea of misunderstandings in our world, sometimes we find a small island of connection. So rare and yet so beautiful to behold.

My Gosh,
When Did I Become Elderly?

The newscaster spoke of the elderly couple who were in an accident on I-93. They were in their early seventies. My wife and I looked at each other, stunned! Why, that's our age; what is this whippersnapper talking about?

Elderly? I know who's elderly, my bud, Irish Tommy. You ask, "How do I know?" He told me so; I have it on tape. Of course, this is the same guy who briskly walks through the streets of New London, or on the track of the Hogan Center for an hour or more, singing Irish drinking songs while listening to his iPod. Try keeping up with him. He's not built for speed, but for endurance in the long haul. He's eighty-six years old.

There is the story of our twenty something granddaughter, who on one of her visits, went with Sweet Nancy to her exercise class. This class is composed of women who are primarily in their seventies. Granddaughter had to take an hour nap when she came home and groaned about her muscle aches the rest of her visit. The next day she let Grandma go alone while she remained in bed.

How many of you have gone to a doctor to ask about a medical issue and hear something like we heard recently, "Well, after all, what do you expect at your age?"

Or the time you were having a conversation with a group of younger people, and you knew you were speaking because your mouth was moving. Yet no one responded. So then we speak louder, but they think we have a hearing problem; or worse, we go silent. I believe one of the issues of the chronologically impaired is they believe they invented sex, drugs, and text messaging. All three impair their ability to complete full sentences.

I suggest we follow the example of Carl, the seventy-eight year old hero of the Disney animation movie, "Up." Russell, a young wilderness explorer, decided to earn his badge helping the elderly, so he continuously badgered Carl trying to be helpful. At the same time, a building project pressures Carl to sell his land, and he doesn't want to. Carl snapped. He refused to let others control his future, and he took Russell on a wild adventure.

We live in a town with scores of elderly people, who in their mid-eighties, still go down-hill skiing, white water rafting, and play a full game of golf walking the course. Our gyms are full of the elderly. There are those still seeking wild adventures in foreign travel. A popular trend is going on a safari in Africa to photograph lions and elephants.

So when you call us elderly, smile, lace up your sneakers, follow us, and try to keep up.   .

Chosen Children

This column is dedicated to all the courageous people who have parented children they have not birthed, but have chosen to raise with their partner and have learned to love them.

When Sweet Nancy and I were first married, our teen-aged children were upset. How upset I learned the day a brick, wrapped in a death threat letter, was thrown through our living room window. Addressed to me, it was thrown from inside, as I was outside. It was signed by all of the children. I thought the phrase, *you have ruined our lives*, was a bit of a stretch, and that given time they would get used to me. My belief wavered when we were served papers from the sheriff's office claiming neglect and child abuse. It took a few days for them to be served, as our sons, six-foot four-inch and six-foot three-inch tall, answered the door. The deputy was sure he was at the wrong house. The third time they snatched the papers and ran inside chortling. Children by nature are skilled at chortling!

When I found out the primary penalty was removing the children from the house, I entered a guilty plea. I started to envision reducing our raw meat expense, turning one of the five bedrooms into a quiet library, and having a place to park in the driveway. When the children discovered they would have to pay their own telephone bill, and live with strangers on the third floor of a tenement, they began to have doubts. When they heard me whistling a happy tune and smiling, they withdrew their charges. We would somehow have to learn to live with each other.

For all of us, it was like living in a foreign country, each tribe with a different history. We held family meetings similar to the US Congress; everyone wanted to talk, and no one wanted to listen. Compromise was a sign of weakness, a betrayal of your tribe. As a leader of the enemy nation, I was addressed as *my mother's husband*, while Sweets was simply called *her*. A truce was reached, as they didn't want to miss family festivities, such as birthday parties and Christmas gifts.

Despite everything, our children grew up, and graduated from high school. Some went to college, some not; some married, some not. Some, despite changing our residence three times, came home again, forcing us to move in the middle of the night, leaving no forwarding address. After a few had children, a tsunami occurred! Within weeks our IQ scores had gained twenty points, they asked for advice, which was quickly forgotten, and we were entrusted with the care of their most precious possession, their CHILDREN.

I must admit they were miffed when we visited and forgot their names; instead called them Jessica's mother or Nathan's father, and brought gifts to the grandchildren they never got when they were young. Sweets and I had no idea that our children would have children so intelligent, attractive, loving, and brimming with personality. Proof that those who struggle through the step-parenting years will be rewarded, or is it vindicated? There is a thread that weaves through our lives as parents or step-parents that ties one generation to the next, and creates something we call My Family.

How sweet it is!

In Case of Emergency

I was born in a taxi-cab. In Philadelphia. The city of brotherly love. It was winter, dark and very cold. This was a story my mother told me every year near my birthday. "Oh God! You almost killed me, nine pounds, big head and broad shoulders. Geez, I almost died." During my growing years, my brother, walking with his friends, would pass me on the street without a nod. Thank God for my older sister. She would pull me to her breast and whisper in my ear, "I love you, Bob." Bob, I learned later, was an old boyfriend from Philadelphia. When I complained to my family, everyone chanted the same maxim, "What doesn't kill you, makes you strong." I thought about changing my name to King Kong.

Thus I learned self-reliance at an early age. This served me well through marriage, divorce, raising children alone, and the endless hurdles we all face in life. Recently I discovered the lessons I learned in childhood may block the wisdom of common sense. When Sweet Nancy asked me to delay my scheduled surgery because she would be away, I said, "Go ahead, I can handle it. It's only minor surgery. I'll arrange to have a trusted friend take me, bring me home, and stay with me until I get settled." I knew I could muddle through even though instructions called for a caretaker. I turned away all offers of help. After all, I am King Kong. I can handle it!

Shortly after Sweets departure the phone rang; it was Susan, our Wonder Daughter, able to jump over five children in a single bound. She spoke lovingly in her gentle, soothing voice: "WHAT! ARE YOU OUT OF YOUR MIND!! There is no such thing as minor surgery, except for the doctor! I know about surgery. I have kids, your grandchildren, may I remind you. Now get on the phone and ask for help!" Until that moment I had no idea Wonder Daughter possessed such abilities as a motivational speaker. It took four hours and twenty people to replace the skills that Sweets would have provided for a stubborn old man in need of assistance.

My eye surgery went well. The Codger Support Team, supervised by Nurses Janice and Vita, were able to wrestle success out of disaster, overpowering my natural tendency to make life harder than necessary. When Sweets returned, I told everyone that my two black eyes and puffy purple cheeks from the procedure were the result of husband abuse. People at church called me Rocky Balboa, and that if my wife hit me, I probably deserved it.

All this activity has me pondering. When you join a gym, take a class, or enter a medical facility, you sign a consent form with a person named who can be contacted in case of emergency. The first listed person is usually our spouse, followed by our adult children, who live down a dirt road in another state. Perhaps it is time for us to return the tools we borrowed from our neighbor, and to talk to that gentleman we have been sitting next to in our church or Rotary meetings. I have my Codger Support team listed on my fridge, as my #1 is not always available. The life you save may be very important to your grandchildren.

Free Range Children

My childhood was a breeding ground for criminal activity. My parents raised me a free range child, something I recently discovered is illegal in a number of states. This past year a couple from Maryland now has a criminal record, since they were caught allowing their children, eight and ten years at the time, to walk without supervision the mile separating the public park from their home. Perhaps many of you suffered the same free range childhood?

Compared to mothers in my town, those parents were saints. I, like most kids in the neighborhood, was forced outside after breakfast to play, and told, "Don't come back unless you are bleeding, or you break your leg." Play was an activity done despite rain, sleet, or snow. If I whined, Mom would raise her claw and growl, "Take a sheet of plastic, wrap it around you in case of rain," thus showing she did care after all.

After school and snack of milk and cookies, I was shoved out the door, and told to play until I heard the dinner bell. My mother had a cowbell, the coach's wife had a whistle, and the Chang family had a gong so loud it could shatter windows. Every night at six, a symphony of sounds called us to follow the kitchen smells home.

Till we heard those supper sounds, everybody in the kid's world roamed about town in packs, noisy and free. The youngest, on metal skates, tightened their Tom McCanns with a silver key. Older kids had bikes of all colors and shapes, with streamers, bells, and horns, most inherited from older brothers, or cobbled together from the dump. Anyone could get a Schwinn or Columbia, but to make your own steed out of spare parts required a skilled craftsman, the ultimate in creative engineering. He was the lead dog; we followed until we fell in love with the rumble of dual exhausts and the highways out of town.

Many of us grew tall during the era of disorganized sports without an adult in sight. We created our versions of sports and games. There was blacktop basketball that went on for days, and was played curb to curb without fouls, nets, or time limits. Twilight football, played with a ball painted white, held together with Day-glo shoelaces, fifteen or more kids to a side. We invented Kill the Kid, which used a dense ball and required players who had the ability to hide bruises from adults.

On rainy days, our sisters convinced us that Monopoly was a contact sport, and after four hours of sitting still, it was. There was so much kid-made fun, the days were never long enough to hold it all. We seldom said we were bored, for if we did, fun stopped, and cleaning our rooms or weeding the garden would smother our days.

The cowbell is long gone, as is the time when we knew our neighbor well enough to tell them we were concerned about their children, instead of calling the police. We thrived and learned self-reliance by creating our own entertainment; let's pass on the same opportunity for our grandchildren.

Get the Candles Darling, Ice Storm Ahead

THOMAS DONNELLY

Get the Candles Darling, Ice Storm Ahead

Prior to the recent December '08 ice storm, we were asked the same question every winter, "Were you here during the Big Ice Storm of 1998 when New London was in the death grip of the Storm of the Century, and we knew the first names of the national guard members keeping watch over the town?

We would look down at our shoes mumbling, "We hadn't moved here yet."

Having survived the storm of '08 without killing each other, we no longer think of ourselves as wimpy Flatlanders, but as almost Woodchucks, and now we can ask newcomers, "Were you here during the Great Ice Storm of the Century in 2008?"

Yet never during our lifetime, has anyone whispered to us any information about the trauma residents struggle with during those nail-biting times. This may explain our fear of loud noises on cold winter nights, not unlike the sound of falling ice, or the stages through which we struggled.

Stage 1 Denial: One partner flips the light switches continually on and off muttering, "Damn power company," while the other grits her teeth.

Stage 2 Snarling: 'Why didn't you buy that generator you talked about?"

"Why didn't you buy more candles?"

"You and your dream of retiring in winter wonderland."

Stage 3 Despair: I start leaving post-it notes around the house for my survivors. "Tell my children I love them. I'm going to die like a lonely ice cube."

174

Stage 4 Jealousy: I start driving the streets, keeping a notebook on who has power, complaining when I arrive home, "Who do they know? Wait until the next town meeting!"

Stage 5 Acceptance: I go back to bed, leaving a copy of our will on the top layer of nine blankets and a note stating, "Do not wake until spring." As I lay there, I hear my wife on the cell phone speaking to the National Guard commander demanding assistance. She then cruelly pulls off my covers singing, "We shall overcome," with the emphasis on we. I feel assured that help is on the way, or at least that I won't die alone.

Winter in New England. When you are young, it is a time for creating babies, as we are all on a frost heave of life. Together we shall overcome—at least until the power comes back on. Maybe it's time to meet the neighbors—the ones with a generator, who will let you take a shower. It could be worse.

Our neighbors could have moved to California, leaving an empty house.

Big Papa

My father was a strong believer in the "children should be seen and not heard" school of fatherhood. Conversation was useless until a youngster reached the age of reason at seven years old. Then you were expected to know the difference between right and wrong, to obey without questions, and to honor your mother and father, as well as other old people. It worked with the first three, why not young Tommy? Enter the Spoiler, my older sister, tired of a life of silence and servitude. She fed me enough information to start a child's resistance movement, and sewed the seeds of a future independent voter.

Ever resourceful, the executive branch adopted strong-arm tactics just short of waterboarding. My sainted mother, the Enforcer, started with a hairbrush, changed to switches from the willow tree, and finally, cattle prods. It was WWII; I listened to nightly radio reports, so I could move my lead soldiers into position. This helped me plan countermoves to her tactics. I began to wear heavy woolen pants year round, along with a padded ski jacket for protection. My mother, a small woman, wore out before I did, forcing her to call for the heavy weapon, Big Papa.

Big Papa boarded an overcrowded train without any climate controls, six days a week, to manage a Woolworth's store in a nearby town. Every day customers haggled with him to lower prices, pushing his job and sanity into the red zone. Trudging home well after dark, he would finally open the door to his sanctuary, only to be greeted by my mother, hands on hips, screaming, "I can't take it anymore; you need to punish YOUR SON!" Even with my protection, I could feel the blows. Big Papa relieved his stress, the Enforcer felt support from her

176

husband, and I learned to tolerate pain. This skill served me well later when I played football, basketball, wrestling, and parenting.

Years later when I became a father, I followed in my father's steps until my sons reached the age of reason. Then I decided to find a better way to raise children. I discovered Doctor Spock. One day I sat my boys down and promised them I would no longer spank them; instead I would send them to their rooms, which happened to be in the dimly lit spider cellar near the furnace. The youngest immediately ran into the backyard near the neighborhood picnic shouting, "My dad says he's not going to beat us anymore, even if I fill up the toilet with coal again." We moved to another town, so I could walk in daylight without fear of a lengthy investigation.

Please remember this is a humor column loosely based on real events. I am sure if you have been a dad involved in the tremendous effort it takes to grow small people into adults, you have your own stories from the closets of your family history. They all begin with "remember when." Perhaps this Father's Day you might want to sit at the table with your wife and kids, and remember the stories from way back, from the beginning of your family's journey till now.

Happy Dad Day, you earned it.

The Power of Small

When I moved to New London, I had my car inspected and serviced at the Exxon station in town. No big deal, but only later as I grew into the community did I realize how special the owner was.

He was a man who had one of the pioneer businesses that helped develop New London, a town of forty-five hundred, into a center for goods and services. Bob Lull was born in Boston during the depression, but at age two moved to New Hampshire until things got better in Bean Town. He never left New London. He grew up in Elkins, and when he came of age, he met and won the heart of a seventh-generation New London gal, his Dottie.

Dottie's roots go back to New London's founding fathers. Claude Goeing, her ancestor, was a Civil War veteran. He earned his living repairing carriages and had a sideline refurbishing violins. His building still stands on the grounds of the New London Historical Society.

Bob worked for Bill Kidder Sr. at the local Shell station, which also supplied gas to the surrounding area. In time Bob formed a partnership with Lloyd Heath that was sealed with a handshake. Both men believed in the old business standard, my word is my bond. Bill Sr., a guardian angel with facial hair, offered advice, encouragement, and gave Bob the courage to start a service station at a time when owning your own business meant working from 7 am until 8 pm, seven days a week. Six years later he bought out his partner. At its peak, there were twelve employees and all received health insurance from Bob, because "it was the right thing to do."

Banks, even at this time, favored larger establishments, which meant in this era before credit cards, that Bob had to carry over a thousand accounts on his own dime. Some were never paid. Employees must have felt he treated them fairly, as some worked there thirty to forty years. Bob smiled warmly as he told stories of these men and his gratitude for sticking with him during hard times. Bob survived the ups and downs of the small business roller coaster for forty-two years! It was a service station with the emphasis on service.

The Lull family has and continues to contribute to the well being of the town and country. Their daughter teaches at the local school, and the sons all have served in the military. They were touched by and encouraged by their parents. Bob and Dottie themselves served as models with their many varied contributions. Bob was a volunteer in the fire department for twenty-years, he served on the zoning board, the budget committee, and bandstand board. Both he and Dottie have long been involved with the New London Boys' Club and the First Baptist Church. Remembering the long hours of owning a small business and raising a family of four children, they went the extra mile and helped to build their community. I felt Bob spent all his adult life giving back. The community has recognized the Lulls by giving them both the Bell and Herbert Swift awards.

This to me is the real New Hampshire advantage, not that neighboring states have a sales tax that we don't. Here the owners live in the community, not another country or state. They raise their families here, send their children to local schools, go to the dump like everyone else. They employ their neighbors, and pay a larger percentage of taxes than corporations who take their profits back to their place of origin. I grew up in a town dependent on big business. When I visited recently, none had remained in the town or even the state.

It's Thanksgiving, so I'm sending a Codger thank you to Bob, and all those small businesses, who have worked long hours to serve us and make our corner of the world a nicer place to live. My own quality of life is so much better here. So when you see Bob, smile. It will make him think he knows you. He's 81 years old; he probably knows your father.

Epilogue: Bob passed away at age 85. The church was filled with people standing in the aisle. It was a tribute to how many lives he had touched; people who had come away with a story and a warm smile, and were living in the town he had helped build.

It Ain't That Bad - Guy Humor

A man and his wife went to see a terminally ill friend in the hospital. John, the friend, was glad to see them both, and told them how important their visit was to him. The wife gave John a hug, asked how he felt, and did he need anything? The husband punched John in the arm and said, "Don't think you are going to get out of paying me the ten dollars you owe me." For the next fifteen minutes the wife watched horrified as the two men traded insults. Welcome to the misunderstood world of guy humor.

During the December 2008 ice storm, I fell down the cellar stairs and broke a rib, as well as collecting numerous cuts and bruises on my journey. On the way to the hospital, I asked the EMT taking my vital signs, "Does this mean my days as a circus clown are over?" It hurt to laugh, but when he chuckled, I didn't feel quite so clumsy. The tension broken, I was able to hear his instructions less defensively.

Randy, from X-ray, who had climbed out of a warm bed at 5 AM to "just do his job," looked a little disheveled. I asked for proof that he was not an imposter. He pointed to his New London Hospital badge and smiled. From that moment on he regaled me with stories of a folk hero called Rusty Wallace, while he gently moved my old broken body around. He made a painful experience less so. I was in the good hands of one of life's everyday heroes.

My male friends and neighbors called me Crash, Evel Knievel, or stunt geezer, among other names not suitable for this column. One of the reasons for our type of humor is that it can take the sting out of something we have done that's really dumb, like falling through an open door in the dark. The flight

181

to the cement floor was thrilling, except for the crash landing at the end.

Perhaps another is that if we can find the humor in a difficult situation we can overcome and solve the problem. It is not that bad - it could be worse. Cultivating a sense of humor allows us to muddle through. It's a guy thing, you'd have to be one.

Day Pass into Women's World

It all started when my big toe ate through my sock—again. In the old days, my mother darned the hole closed. When I asked Sweets to sew the hole like the old days, she rolled her eyes and said, "That's why it's called the old days. They're gone forever." Since I cut my own toenails, I asked, "What should I do to save my socks?" She told me I needed a pedicure, but I turned that down, because I have had enough surgery to last a lifetime. Wives should not slap their thigh, laugh at their husbands until they cry, and call all their girlfriends to chortle about people with facial hair.

Eventually I made an appointment online with the Happy Feet Nail Salon. At the appointed hour, I entered a large room full of women in conversation, which stopped as soon as I came in. On one side was a long row of thrones with water troughs at their feet. The other side had a wall of mirrors above old-fashioned white school desks, with desktops covered with sandpaper sticks. For woodworking I wondered? A small girl, looking like an eighth grader, emerged from the group. "Can I help you? Did you come to pick up your wife, or are you looking for the bathroom?" Uh-oh, I had stumbled into a women's world where all men are strangers.

When I informed the eighth grader I had an appointment, she called a sixth grader with an unpronounceable name. I guess she was their toenail-cutting specialist. She wore what I noticed was the business uniform for all, a black tee shirt, ripped jeans with sequins, blue sandals, and a blue smart phone at half-mast in her back pocket. To complete her outfit, she wore her jet black hair pulled back at the top of her head, and held together with a yellow rubber band. This caused her hair to spike in a fan. She never looked up and spoke from behind her hand. "Sit down, put feet in trough," she ordered.

Perched high on my designated throne, hidden among a long row of women, I watched the black shirted sixth graders grab a hose and fill the troughs at our feet with hot water. My feet glowed red in the shadows. "Feet up," she ordered. My child had a plastic fishing box next to her, from which she extracted tiny hedge clippers, white wall tire scrubbers, and lotions that resembled soap from dispensers in public bathrooms. For the next 20 minutes she cut, scrubbed, and rubbed until my feet felt like they could walk on water. At the halfway point, she pushed a button on the throne, causing my back to melt, as I prayed in a long forgotten language on my way to heaven.

At the end, my child whispered in my ear, "Time you get up now, or should I call 911?" Before giving me my bill, she showed me pictures of her children. Oh no, sixth graders here have children? I am not ready for this world. It was wonderful to spend an hour visiting a women's world, but I had to go home, eat a bucket of greasy fried chicken, shake my fist, and shout as I watched twelve hours of violent sports in order to regain my manliness. Sweets asked me if I had my toenails colored, but I couldn't decide between gunmetal gray or pigskin brown. Never grow so old you miss a new adventure.

May I Suggest

The page has turned; another year has faded into memory, but has opened a path to a new adventure. I feel a sense of sadness when I hear people speak as if all our best days were behind us, those days when we were a lawyer, a doctor, or set a record with the crowd cheering. That time might be the birth of a child, or a special present you keep hidden in the attic of your mind, when you felt so loved you couldn't sleep. It could be the times when you taught young students a skill, and in their mastery of it, you made a difference in their entire future.

May I suggest to you, there is more, despite the aches, pains, and losses you may have suffered which have shaped you this hour. So please don't hang your happiness hat on age. There are those younger than you and I, who sink into deep despair over election results, the final standing of their favorite sports team, or today's Dow Jones average. A crabby disposition crosses all boundaries and can affect the air we breathe, no matter how sweet the air.

May I suggest, and you will know the truth of what I speak, when I offer to you the laughter of a grandchild who runs across the room of loneliness to be held in the warm circle of your arms. You may remember the phone call from an old friend that neither miles nor time can erase, as you walked together along the memories. He or she whispered how much your time together meant. It may be your turn to reach out and call someone across the miles, and for a moment, just a moment in time, to look forward instead of back.

I came from a family that viewed the world through dark glasses. I learned destructive criticism at an early age. Trust was a business term, having nothing to do with relationships. Positive thinking was for people who lacked a firm grip on reality. Life was hard, and you'd better get used to it and not expect too much. Can you see how we might have been a real joy to have around?

One of the ways I change my story is through music. There is a song, "May I Suggest," composed by Susan Werner, written for the dark days of the winter times of our lives. It has helped me turn my head in a new direction. Sweets and I heard it at a concert given by a group called Red Molly. The crowd left in holy silence. We had been moved to a new place. You can see or hear them on YouTube or view Susan Werner's version. To get the full flavor, I recommend you download the words and read them like a prayer. The following is the end of the song, and may speak to our time of life.

"To see how very short the endless days will run,
And when they're gone,
And when the dark descends,
Oh, we'd give anything for one more hour of light,
And I suggest,
This is the best part of your life."

It's a new day. Let us not waste that hour.

The Old Man
and the Dark Haired Girl

During our tarnished golden years, Sweet Nancy and I travel the country to bask in the proud glow of our family's college graduations. We seldom are able to sit together. Recently, I boarded a plane bound for Montana with my iPad loaded with three books; one for waiting at the airport, another for the long flight, and a spare for runway delays.

Finally seated on the plane, I had just opened my iPad, when I noticed my seat- mate. She was a young, brown skinned woman, wearing day-glow lipstick, a silver ring piercing each nostril, and a ring capped by a green stone piercing her eyebrow. All this framed by long black hair covering her shoulders. Nothing in common with a balding old man with limited social skills.

I had just read the first page, when I noticed my companion reach down into a rainbow colored bag and pull out a square object. With reverent care she peeled back the silk cover decorated with butterflies and flowers to reveal a book. A book I had read years ago, a book about warrior women. I knew about warrior women. All the women in my family are strong women, even the pets. She was surprised that a grandfather had read such a book. I closed my iPad.

Jenny is twenty-one; I am inching close to eighty. She was part of a team of college students working at Yellowstone National Park during summer break to earn money for college. What could we possibly find to talk about? We lived in two different worlds. Yet, we found enough in each other to talk the length of the flight, two hours. The shortest distance between two people often is a good story.

This is but a small drop of her fascinating story. "I am an immigrant kid raised with a love of books. My parents were both university professors in Nicaragua when the Contras seized power and shut down the schools. They immigrated to Calgary Canada, unable to speak the language, without a job, with little money, and they did not know a soul. They were very brave!

"My sisters and I were given opportunities never available to them. My sisters are university-trained engineers. But I did not want to be an engineer, so I appealed to my father. He surprised me when he gave me his permission to "become the one who helps the many."

She went on, "I am in my second year at university in Alberta. I want to research and discover ways to help children and their parents suffering from the trauma of losing their home from natural disasters. I believe I owe it to my parents to help others."

During our time together, we traded stories sewn together like a roadmap covering the journey of our lives, one a bright beginning, the other entering twilight time.

Someone recently asked, when is someone elderly? I wish I had been quick enough to respond, when we tell stories from our lives and no one listens. Despite a well-lived life we now feel invisible. We live at a time and place where people talk to their phones more than their families, where families live like strangers in the same house, and our divided government has forgotten whom it represents.

This experience of two so different people coming together to reach out to each other to learn about their lives gives me hope. While waiting with Sweets for our luggage, Jenny ran up and hugged me as she whispered in my ear, "Thank you for listening to me. Hardly anyone ever does; you gave me a gift."

I guess the elderly and the young have more in common that I had ever imagined.

A Story for Christmas

A long time ago in a place far away, there lived a woman, who every weekday sat with the same ladies at the senior center to eat lunch. She said very little, and spoke only when spoken to. She sat at the very end of the table, with her head down, her body bent and twisted by arthritis. I sat next to her, and asked if she had a favorite Christmas, since it was the season.

This is what she told me: "We were a family of acrobats. There was a special Christmas during WWII, when my mother, father, and I were part of a USO tour in the Pacific. Somehow we became separated from the larger tour group, and were headed for a different island. I was young, small, and pretty skinny." She let her oversized winter coat drop to the floor.

"We were making slow progress, because of the wind and the rain, well, they were something fierce. We reached the island, I don't remember its name, toward the end of the afternoon. We couldn't get ashore, and were forced to go to the other side of the island before it got dark. We were welcomed by a couple of marines who hadn't expected us. They said there was no electricity, but as we were here, they'd fix something up. It seemed that the guys had not been home in a longtime, and since it was almost Christmas, they were feeling low. How could we say no?

"Later that night we were driven with our equipment to an open field, which had a freshly made mound of dirt in its center that was flattened on top. Around the mound were parked an assortment of Jeeps and trucks tilted upward, all with their lights on, and their engines running. Somehow that night, we performed in those headlights. My parents tumbled, rode bicycles, did handstands, and my father told terrible jokes that produced much laughter. Then it was my turn on the wire." When she said this, Florence stood, and she raised her arms above her head, her pain momentarily forgotten. "I performed as never before, with jumps, spins, and somersaults. At the end, I was dripping wet. There was silence! Then, shouts, whistles, and applause. For one moment I was a star. Just for that one moment! I was a 14-year old girl; I couldn't fight in a war. This was my gift to the boys, and they loved it!"

She picked up her coat, sat down, pulling her coat around herself. The women at the table sat stunned, their mouths open. All these years Florence had a wonderful story hidden inside her waiting to be told. The women asked why they had never heard this story before. Her reply, "Nobody ever asked."

In ancient times, when I was young, we would look for ways to get into the spirit of Christmas. When the kids were small, we went to children's concerts or school plays. It gets a wee bit harder when grandchildren are so far away. Last year my Montana family gave me one of the best presents ever! Every week, I received an e-mail from someone in the family, including our granddaughter who was in college. Every week it started, "Dear Boppa, Let me tell you a story from my life..." A story shortens the distance between two people.

We all have a holiday story hidden within us. Maybe instead of Christmas, it's about Hanukkah. Why not ask someone, a friend, a grandchild, a sibling, or even a stranger waiting in line at the supermarket: "Do you have a story?" Then wait for the reply, and if they have none, tell them one of yours.

Merry Christmas and Happy Hanukkah,

Ole Snowcodger and Sweet Nancy

THOMAS DONNELLY

Who are they?

The Codger, AKA Thomas Donnelly, has held a number of jobs including factory work and heavy equipment operations before becoming a family addictions counselor.

Sweets, AKA Nancy Donnelly, was a nurse for many years, then became an ordained minister, specializing in chaplaincy. She served in hospitals and hospice.

They found each other after their spouses died, and formed a blended family with ten children. They are blessed with thirteen grandchildren and three great-grandchildren. Their motto is "We may be old, but we are bold."
They live in New London, New Hampshire, and snowbird in Fairhope, Alabama.

Bill Bastille and Janet Moore- our readers, thanks for your help.

Cover photograph taken by Vincent Lawson, Mobile, Alabama. Vincentsphotographs@gmail.com